Guilt-Proof Parenting

How to be a better parent through those tough teen years

Guilt-Proof Parenting

How to be a better parent through those tough teen years

Priscilla de Garcia
&
Robert Wolenik

 Writer's Digest Books Cincinnati, Ohio

93 92 91 90 89 88   5 4 3 2 1

Library of Congress Cataloging-in-Publication Data

deGarcia, Priscilla Partridge, 1942-
  Guilt-proof parenting/Priscilla Partridge deGarcia, Robert Wolenik.
  p. cm.
  Includes index.
  ISBN 0-89879-304-1
  1. Parenting. 2. Parent and child. 3. Child psychology. I. Wolenik, Robert. II. Title.
HQ755.8.D44 1988
649'.1—dc19   87-33972
                                                                           CIP

Design by Judy Allan.

For Rita, Chad, Tim, Paulette, David, Lloyd, Manny, Pedro and our eight children.

Priscilla

CONTENTS

You know you're guilt-ridden every time your child runs into any kind of problem, but do you know where that guilt comes from? A society that always blames parents, an unrealistic view of what children are really like, even your own anger when your child misbehaves can heap those feelings of guilt on your shoulders.

Not every teenage trouble can be traced to poor toilet training or some other parental mistake. Explore nine other major reasons for turbulence in the teenage years.

A child's natural selfishness, so important in the early years, can cause a teenager to be inconsiderate, even rude. Learn how to use painful experiences to help your teen outgrow this.

Sometimes a parent's personality and that of the child simply don't match well. A short questionnaire will help you identify your child's personality traits to determine if some of your difficulties are the result of a bad fit.

Part 2
FIVE WAYS TEENS
MISBEHAVE   *123*

PREFACE

I first met Dr. Priscilla deGarcia as a client of hers. I have three sons, now aged sixteen, fourteen, and ten. They are good children, but they are a handful—several hands full. In fact, at that time things seemed to be getting completely out of hand. My wife and I felt we had messed up because the kids behaved badly—sometimes grunting at us instead of talking, usually not following directions or rules, acting disrespectful, and, in general, making mayhem out of our household. To me it was perfectly obvious I was a terrible parent.

At the time, my wife and I felt we had tried everything. We had talked until we were hoarse. I had yelled at the kids and even, on one occasion, had taken the "back of my hand" and given the two older boys each a few whacks. That really wasn't the answer. The guilt I felt after those kinds of punishments convinced me that I couldn't do it again. I wasn't going to be that kind of parent.

Obviously, my wife and I were doing something wrong, so I went to Dr. deGarcia for help.

What I learned from Dr. deGarcia is that it usually takes two to create a problem, both the parent *and* the child. I learned that the boys were responsible for their actions and that they created at least half the environment in which they lived. I learned how to treat them so that they felt better about themselves and showed respect for both my wife and me. In the end, I learned how to go from simply being a loving parent full of guilt to being a loving, yet effective good parent.

I also saw that Dr. deGarcia's approach was far different from any other that I had read or heard about. She didn't blame me or find fault with what I did or had done. Quite the contrary, she removed my own feelings of guilt. She helped me cope with my regrets for those many times I had not handled the children as I later felt I should have. She showed me that children can be manipulative and how to deal with that fact.

I've since discovered that Dr. deGarcia is at the leading edge of a revolution in handling children called the "family systems" approach. In her practice, Dr. deGarcia found that parents and children got better by dealing with the entire family in group interactions rather than by dealing with one person.

Dr. deGarcia developed her approach earning her master's and doctorate degrees in counseling psychology at the University of Southern California while married and raising three children. She has worked as a guidance counselor in public schools and as a teacher and director of a re-entry center for adults going back to school. She founded the Alive Center and later the AIM Center, where she practiced and trained therapists in family counseling. She has also promoted this approach while instructing counselors and therapists in the master's programs at California Lutheran University and California State University at Northridge.

Dr. deGarcia is unusual in that she openly discusses her own experiences with her clients. She has been divorced and remarried, becoming a stepmother. This led her to work with "blended" families. During her twenty-three years of professional life, she has dealt with many different ethnic groups and with people from widely varied backgrounds and educational levels.

Her goal is to share her knowledge and personal experiences so people can see that all of us have problems and that we can learn from one another. Toward that end Dr. deGarcia became a national speaker, regularly writes articles for newspapers and magazines, and has her own radio and TV talk shows.

Being a professional writer with fifty-three published books, I naturally suggested to Dr. deGarcia that she put her philosophy and her therapy into book form. I pointed out that there were literally millions of parents, perhaps like you, who could benefit from what she had to say but who had no chance of ever getting the benefits of her therapy on a personal, firsthand basis.

She agreed, and this book is the result. I think it will be a lifesaver to a lot of loving, caring parents like you.

A SPECIAL NOTE ABOUT THIS BOOK

When you read this book, don't expect the same old bland generalizations that have been rewritten since the Baby Boom began. Expect something new, something revolutionary.

Also, don't expect to receive simple answers to complex questions. I can recall a friend who was having trouble with his teenager. One day he dropped the child off at a psychologist and said, "Here she is. The troubles are A, B, and C. Fix her!" It just doesn't work that way.

This book will help if you are having problems with your children. But it will not point the finger of blame either at the child or at you and say, "There is the problem!" Rather, it will do something that few books thus far have done—it will explain the complex relationship between parents and children.

The truth, if we dare to admit it, is that very few of us really understand children. Just because we were once children ourselves, because we can biologically have children, and because we must economically support them, does not automatically mean we understand them psychologically. In fact, when most parents finally do learn what their children are about, it comes as a shock.

This book will help explain *why* your children act as they do, particularly as teenagers. As never before, you will see your sons and daughters in a new light—as they truly are. Of course, along the way we will also make specific suggestions and offer guidance and rules.

WHAT YOU CAN EXPECT WHEN YOU READ THIS BOOK

For the vast majority of us, child raising involves a lot of guilt, a lot of self-blame, and a lot of paralyzing fear that we are harming rather than helping the child.

This book will help change that for you. Once you see another perspective of what's really happening between parent and child, the bad feelings you may have been harboring about yourself will start to melt away. You will begin to realize that you probably did not cause all the problems and may even be blameless much of the time.

You can expect this book to help remove the *fear* and *guilt* you feel when dealing with your children and to transform your helplessness into positive action. This book will forever change how you think of your children. With this insight, you will find yourself able to take positive, effective action, to find better solutions for the problems and challenges of raising teenagers. You will find enormous power is available to you, because you will start to shed your inhibiting feelings of guilt. You will stop blaming yourself and will move forward toward becoming a more effective parent.

What's best of all, after reading this book and acting on it, you will once again be able to love your children in that deep and fulfilling way you've always wanted to love them.

Robert Wolenik

INTRODUCTION: UNDERSTANDING GUILT

Is the parent to blame for the child? In our society the answer has always been, "Yes!"

If we see a mother shake a child in the grocery store, our natural reaction is to consider her a bad, perhaps even abusive parent. But maybe that child has been testing her mother all day and the mother has tried everything to make her behave. Maybe if we were the parent in that spot, we would have done the exact same thing. Yet, somehow, we never give the parent the benefit of the doubt.

This tendency to blame the parents is particularly acute with teenagers. Often, parents who feel they have done a good job find that when their child becomes a teen, something suddenly goes wrong. The child may do poorly at school, be antisocial, or even run away from home or become involved with drugs. Who feels the guilt? Who is blamed? The parents.

Society is particularly quick to point an accusing finger at the parent who works, who is divorced, who doesn't have much time to devote to the child. Schools, therapists, and other adults place so much emphasis on parental responsibility that frequently even the child ends up blaming the parents for his or her own problems.

Parents blame themselves, too. Most are struggling to do the best job they can, but the teen years can be a time of misgivings and self-doubt for the parents: "We failed. We weren't there when we were needed. We didn't give enough love and support."

All this finger-pointing can cause even loving, well-meaning parents to be debilitated by feelings of guilt and failure. They start doubting themselves and their decisions. They may feel they've lost control of their teens, and ask themselves over and over the gut-wrenching question, "Where did I go wrong?"

At some point, parents have to stop blaming themselves. At some point, they have to insist the child take responsibility for his or her actions. Parents have to draw a line and say, "We did the best we could." *Guilt-Proof Parenting* shows you how to draw that line and stop blaming yourself so you can evaluate behavior more fairly. Is the immature 10-year-old who pouts and throws a tantrum only reflecting parental mistakes or is he demonstrating personal choice? Is the teenager who gets bad grades, who goes out and gets drunk every weekend doing so because the parents failed? Or is it because she's being pressured by friends who enjoy getting bad grades and drinking?

Guilt-Proof Parenting does not justify bad parenting. But it does remove blame from good parents who have tried everything only to see things still come out wrong. And it gives parents many hints and clues on how getting rid of guilt can improve their parenting. Most important, it shows that kids need to take responsibility, too.

WHERE GUILT BEGINS

You may not have realized it, but you probably entered parenthood with an unrealistic view of children, a romantic vision like the following: "Children come with clouds trailing behind them, as perfect gifts from God. They are always good. They know what they need as do all of nature's creatures. If we just give them their way, they will unfold into very good people."

This perception usually lasts only a short time after the baby is brought home from the hospital. Then reality creeps in.

The baby is demanding. The baby won't sleep, won't eat, or won't stop crying. The baby wets and poops all the time. Sometimes the baby might even seem like a terror.

But then there are also those times when the baby is cuddly, sweet, warm, precious, and unbelievably lovable. How could anyone feel anger toward such a wonderful gift? What kind of people would have negative thoughts about this sweet, innocent child?

Undoubtedly you've experienced both these feelings—the wonder of the child *and* the anger at the tyranny of the child. If you're like most of us, you've felt not just a little guilt over these confusing emotions.

The reasoning usually goes like this: I'm supposed to love and cherish my children, so why do I sometimes feel anger and resentment toward them? Loving parents shouldn't get burning mad or show hostility toward their kids. Loving parents should never get into a rage over what their children have done. Loving parents should always listen to their children. They are always there for their kids. Loving parents should always show love and warmth for their children.

No one can fit the ideal all of the time. When you aren't what you consider the perfect parent, what does that say about you? If you get angry and resentful toward your children, does it mean that you don't love them enough? If they do bad things or get involved in serious problems, does that mean that you failed them as parents? Perhaps you have made mistakes, but all of us do. That doesn't mean you don't love your children or that you're a failure.

If you believe that children come to you perfect and that every mistake they make is your fault, you're in a real dilemma. On the one hand you have an idealistic notion of children (mostly foisted on you by society). On the other hand, as you begin parenting, you discover that you just can't live up to your (or society's) expectations. Most likely, instead of realizing that neither children or parents are as perfect as all that, you blame yourself. That's one way guilt begins.

Guilt as Anger Turned Inward

The cycle of guilt that begins when parents feel bad for resenting their baby's constant demands continues to grow as the child does. When an older child misbehaves, parents quite naturally feel angry. Gestalt theorists feel that parents do not know how to accept angry feelings toward their children, so instead of dealing with the anger, they tell themselves they shouldn't feel the way they actually do. A good parent wouldn't get so mad. A good parent would be more loving, understanding, and caring. Thus parents end up feeling guilty that they're not better parents.

TAKING ON TOO MUCH

Another reason many parents feel guilty is that they take on too much responsibility—holding themselves accountable for *everything* their children do or become. They do this because of the belief that children are made, not born.

Most parents believe they are given a wonderful new child and then mold him or her into an adult. That, they think, is their greatest responsibility in life—the creation of the child and ultimately that adult from the infant.

This belief is sometimes called the theory of "tabula rasa," or blank slate. It holds that babies come with unfilled minds and unfilled personalities that their parents then fill up. The child is like a vessel into which they pour ideas and personality.

Parents who believe their children come to them as blank slates leave themselves open to an immense load of guilt. If they create their children "from scratch," so to speak, then they're to blame for every character flaw, every mistake the child makes.

But is the blank slate theory really true?

Remember the very moment you first saw your own baby? You will recall that you immediately recognized the special ways she or he was different from other babies. The differences might have included such things as the amount of hair or the hair texture. It certainly was the shape of the face, the hands, the torso, the feet. It was soon a hundred other unique traits. As the baby grew older, these traits became even more defined so that your child instantly became recognizable from any other.

It's indisputable that every baby is different on the outside. Why, therefore, should we suppose that it's any different inside? If children have different external appearances, why wouldn't they have different internal "appearances"? Why wouldn't they each have their own special temperament?

Predetermined Personalities

Just ask any parents who have more than one child. They know and can tell you that each came into the world with different movements, different eating patterns, different personality traits. The first baby may have liked to be held, the second may not. One child may have come into the world not really excited about eating and may have had to be coaxed to be suckled. Another couldn't get enough milk.

Consider identical twins. Studies have shown that such twins reared apart are often more similar to each other and have more similar temperaments and educational skills and IQs than siblings raised in the same household. Or consider the case of the child who crosses his toes and tilts his head exactly as his father, who he's never seen.

All these children are exhibiting traits they were born with, not traits they learned from their parents.

While nearly all parents think of their children as a tabula rasa—a blank slate—mothers and fathers also instinctively recognize definite personalities with which their children are born (which become even more distinct and defined and sometimes more difficult to deal with) as the children mature.

This apparent contradiction is at the heart of many child-rearing problems. Although parents sense it, intellectually most refuse to admit that children, like trees, essentially grow on their own. Some will turn into tall sequoias and others will be lovely willows. Some will have a rough bark and others will be smooth. Some will spread their leaves across vast areas, while others will lead small, slender lives.

Yes, water and fertilizer will help, but what a tree will become is largely in the nature of the tree. It will be what it will be. So it is with children. Parents don't grow children. Children grow themselves. You can help or hinder the process, but you're not fully to blame for every negative thing that happens to them or for every negative personality trait they sprout any more than you're to blame if you plant a seed you think will be a rosebush and it turns out to be a prickly pear instead. (By the same reasoning, you can't take full credit for everything good about your child, either.)

Where Does Personality Come From?

If the parents don't create the child's personality, where *does* it come from? Is it nature or nurture? Is it learned or inborn? There are several theories. Some experts say personality may be determined by genes, the same way eye color is. Some studies have suggested that what the mother eats during pregnancy can have a great deal to do with the way children develop. Or it may be the case that the child learns personality in the womb from what it hears and feels. Or perhaps some other explanation is more fitting.

What's important is not to get muddled down in theory and blame. Parents need to stop looking for someone or something to be the culprit for children's actions. What's important is to be realistic and recognize that just as the baby has a defined body, so too does it have a definite personality that is present from birth.

Ultimately it really doesn't matter why children have unique personalities from birth. What matters is that parents recognize this phenomenon. Once you do, then you can begin to understand that children have much more to do with what happens to them than most of us have been led to believe. (That's not to say that children totally control their environment. They don't, any more than we do. But they do affect it with their temperament. For example, if they fuss, wake up constantly, are cranky and irritable, they produce stress in those around them. As a result, they tend to grow in a stressful environment that they contributed to creating.)

Once you become realistic and accept the idea that children are born with definite personalities, you then can begin to tear down the structure that has been housing your guilt. If they came to you with defined personalities, then you can't be totally to blame for the problems that seem to mature during adolescence or the personality traits that seem to appear from nowhere.

You've been given a child—a beautiful, wonderful, *defined* child. It's yours to help develop, not to mold. It's yours to teach, not to give it intelligence. It's yours to nurture for what it is, not to make it into something else. These are subtle but critically important differences.

Personality Traits are Lifelong

Since the child is born with a defined personality, specific traits don't really appear suddenly at age thirteen, although it may seem that way. They develop as the child grows. Traits of infants develop into traits of young children that expand to become teen characteristics. Young adults develop even further the personalities with which they were born.

The child who can't get enough to eat as a baby is often the hungry, always-eating adult. The child who constantly needs to be played with may be the adult who fights to keep our attention. The child who loves to cuddle and hug may become the warm, affectionate adult.

The personality traits of children endure. Children don't outgrow the personality traits with which they are born any more than they outgrow the color of their eyes or the complexion of their skin. They enlarge and expand upon them. So the personality traits that seem so surprising in your teenager were there in the beginning. Children do try on (in the sense of trying on new clothes) new behaviors as they begin to test their power, to get their wings. But this is not the same thing as getting a new personality.

This line of reasoning is supported by recent research. More and more we are finding that persons who are addicted to drugs, alcohol, or food may have a biological bent for addiction. Some studies have suggested that even a tendency toward antisocial or criminal behavior may be innate—that is, within the personality of the child.

To put it in perspective, the child's development is only in part the result of the nurturing and the parenting you give him or her. It is also due to that defined personality with which she or he came into the world. You are given a certain amount of material with which to work. You can modify and enhance it, but you cannot change it into something different.

TEENAGE SHOCK

The shock of discovering that your child is not the person you thought he or she was is most dramatic and profound when that child becomes a teenager. Parents say things such as, "It's as though there suddenly were a stranger in my house" or "He just walks around like an animal grunting all the time. I can't believe it's my child!" or "She hangs out with a bad crowd, she won't come home when I tell her, and I hate to admit it, but I think she may be experimenting with drugs. Where did it all come from?"

Although you may have seen and ignored signs here and there along the way, it often isn't until the child becomes a teen that what seems to be a new personality suddenly appears.

How could this happen? How could the cuddly little baby you brought into this world, and into whose raising you poured your soul and heart, become so angry, arrogant, and insolent?

You expected something so different. Now the child seems to be having a new problem every day. You see your lovely child with green and pink spiked hair, with a ring in his or her ear, wearing wild clothes, getting poor grades. If it weren't your child, it would be comical. But it is your child.

Finding the Person to Blame

Inevitably, as you see what your child has "suddenly become," you try to find someone to blame. As a rule, you usually only find yourself.

This is only natural. If, like most parents, you believe that you are creating the person, then even from your child's infancy you've been blaming yourself for your children's problems.

When the infant has colic, you blame yourself for not giving her a better diet. When the two-year-old throws a tantrum, you feel guilty for not paying more attention to the baby's needs. When the seven-year-old can't seem to make friends at school or when the eleven-year-old has trouble with his teacher, you feel that it's your fault.

So when the teenager suddenly appears as an alien from another planet in your child's body, you blame yourself. You've probably heard the generalizations about "stages" and about "teen rebellion," but that doesn't really seem to help when you're dealing with your child. Most loving parents simply can't help but feel it's their fault.

When the child messes up, you feel that you are to blame. After all, who else is there to blame? Who else is responsible? Good parents feel that they raised their children and, therefore, must bear the responsibility for their children's actions. The parent is *guilty!*

Or at least, so goes the rationale with the vast majority of parents.

IT'S NOT ALWAYS YOUR FAULT

In this book we are going to be taking a different tack. We are going to look at child behavior in a way that for many readers may be revolutionary. We are going to look at the child's responsibility in all of this at any age, but particularly during the teen years. We're also going to look at outside influences that help shape a child, such as peer pressure and adult authorities outside the home. You will see that loving parents are not always at fault when they have children who mess up.

The reality is that a child's problems are *not* always your fault. In fact, it may be no one's fault when children give parents trouble or turn out badly. It may be just life and living. It's the process of the child trying to detach himself or herself from the parents in order to live independently and as an individual rather than a carbon copy of them.

You'll see how to identify and understand who the players are and what their parts are in your own life's drama. You'll see just how unrealistic many of your notions about children are and what you can realistically expect from your children and from yourself. In the process, you will come to see more clearly how to solve problems that now seem overwhelming. One step at a time, you will move forward with a little less guilt and a little more objectivity.

Most important, you'll begin to see that parents are not always to blame—that parents need to throw off that shroud of guilt that many take on so readily. We will see that very often the problems that children have are caused not by the fact that their parents love them too little, but by the fact that they love them too much. Loving from the heart is only half the battle. Parents must love from the brain as well.

LOVING FROM THE BRAIN

You have to remember how important love is. It's the one ingredient that is vital, a necessity in any family situation. Without it, things will never work out.

It is important to love your children and your spouse's children. It is important to tell your children that you love them. *But your love must not be mindless. You must carefully consider how you show that love.*

Do you show it by *simply* being caring, understanding, and giving? Is this all that the child needs?

Or are you smart? Do you show your love by understanding your child? Do you act from the head instead of just from the heart?

When you deal with children you must analyze what is really going on. Children don't act the way they do for no reason. They are smart, thinking people.

Understand that most incidents do not occur in a vacuum. People are usually reacting to something. Try to figure out what. Try to see it from other points of view. Try to communicate.

Love is wonderful, love is necessary, but every good parent must also be a thoughtful one.

HANDLING FEAR

Some parents are actually *afraid* of their children, particularly their teenage children. Or they may be afraid of losing their children's love if they're strict or make an unpopular decision. These fears are commonplace in many families, but few parents will admit their fears.

When parents react to their children based on their own fears, they may hesitate to discipline a kid who has misbehaved, afraid that the child will be angry or will withdraw. If a child senses this fear, he or she may take advantage of it. One teen may break curfew and threaten to run away if she's punished. Another may scream that he hates his parents when they won't give him permission for a weekend excursion. Instead of facing disappointments and responsibilities, these children get used to having their own way and fail to grow up.

So if you experience fear, you must learn to overcome it. Ask yourself, what is the greater act of love? To give way to this fear, to give in to the children and give up control? Or to be strong regardless of your fear, to refuse to be manipulated by the children and ultimately force them to experience the reality of life?

Remember, the pain of a child, any child, facing reality and not getting his or her way is minor compared with the loss suffered by failing to mature.

A FEW WORDS OF CONSOLATION

You're right, no one ever told you how hard it was going to be. No one said beforehand that you could never be sick, tired, or allowed to sleep in again. No one said that no matter how bad you felt, you would still be the one to crawl to the stove to heat the soup for the children. No one told you that the child's energy increases as you age and your energy decreases.

Even if someone had told you, would you have believed them? Probably not. Most new parents are idealistic, believing that they're special and that their children will of course turn out well.

Can you remember when you were young and said that you would never do what your parents did to you? You would just love and be positive and supportive to your kids. You would never be judgmental or critical.

But, with experience comes wisdom and reality. When your children were babies, would you have listened to the stories of teenagers' parents? Would you have believed it could happen to you?

It really doesn't matter if you knew what was coming or not. In spite of it all, very few parents would give their children back!

You have to remember that you did not have children to "screw them up." You had children because you thought you could do a fairly good job, maybe even a better job than your own parents. You have to remember that parenting is a unique experience, which, though humbling, builds character and patience. You have to remember that you have to forgive yourself for being human and sometimes making mistakes.

When you can do that, you will have taken the first step toward a happier, more effective method of handling those tough teenage years. You'll be well on the way to guilt-proof parenting.

PART

1

Nine Reasons for Teenage Turbulence

To become a guilt-proof parent, you have to recognize that the problems that come with the teenage years are not always due to bad parenting. You have to let yourself off the hook.

Part I will help you do that. It'll show you some of the other influences on a teenager and how important those influences can be. You'll see the effects of the teen's own makeup—the natural selfishness that comes with youth, a personality that just doesn't match the parents' personalities very well, even biological problems such as allergies and chemical imbalances. You'll learn about the influences of others, such as siblings, peers, school authorities, and counselors. You'll take a look at causes that are situational, like having divorced or working parents.

In short, you'll learn that it's not always your fault.

1
Narcissism

Narcissus, son of Cephisus, the Greek river god, was blessed with extremely good looks. He was so handsome that a great many girls fell in love with him and vied for his attention. However, he was so involved with himself that he didn't pay attention to the maidens. The nymph Echo was so hurt by his coldness that she faded away, all but her voice.

When the gods discovered this, they were angered. To punish Narcissus for his treatment of Echo and others, they made him go down to a clear pool. When he looked into the reflective waters, he saw his own face, and he instantly fell in love with his reflection. Narcissus couldn't bear to leave the reflection and stayed at the pool until he died. Then the gods transformed him into the flower that bears his name.

A parent recently watched his teenager open a package of cookies, then sit down and eat every one. The parent asked, "How come you ate them all?"

The teenager replied, "I was hungry." To which the parent continued, "But you could have eaten other things. We have apples and cheese and lots of things. Don't you think your brother and sister might have liked some of the cookies?"

At the mention of siblings, the teenager looked surprised. Then he shrugged his shoulders and said, "So?"

This kind of self-centered attitude, which we have termed *narcissism,* is probably the single most significant psychological factor affecting the actions of kids (as well as adults) in our culture. In children, narcissism is a natural attribute and, if recognized and handled properly, a healthy one. But, as in the case of the Greek youth, narcissism can be harmful if not kept in bounds.

It's vital that as a parent you realize just how much teenagers are motivated by this attitude. If you don't, you may not fully understand why your kids act like they do and may start to feel that you're at fault when your children do things that don't take others into account. You may also find it difficult to help your kids outgrow their narcissism.

To understand narcissism in teenagers, let's first look at how it affects our society in general.

NARCISSISM IN OUR CULTURE

Narcissism is nowhere more evident than in our use of the word *freedom.* Ours is the "Land of the Free." But what do we mean by *freedom?*

The original meaning was quite clear. Freedom was an individualistic ideal. Our founders were strong individuals who said no to all kinds of oppression by striking out for themselves in a wild and strange land. Their goals were independence from foreign domination and self-reliance.

But today that meaning has changed. For most Americans it has come to be, "I want what I want, when I want it!" Over the years our magnificent heritage of individualism and self-reliance has been somehow transformed into, "Hurrah for me! The hell with you!" Ours is a narcissistic culture.

The result is that we as a culture tend to revere selfish behavior. If you have any doubts about this, just study television commercials—they almost universally appeal to our narcissism.

The selfishness in our culture comes from a lack of psychological character. We tend to seek *instant* relief or gratification in the face of pain or crisis. We don't have the psychological character to have patience. When placed in painful or crisis situations, we often make illogical or immature decisions, going for the "fast fix." This often takes the form of drug abuse, alcohol abuse, extramarital affairs, overeating, overscheduling, or some other form of abusive behavior.

PARENTING IN A NARCISSISTIC CULTURE

This cultural narcissism causes problems for parents of teenagers. It can blind them to the problems of a child's narcissism. As a result, selfishness that would never be tolerated in an altruistic society may be accepted here. For example, if a teenager takes advantage of a terrible blizzard to make extra money shoveling sidewalks, he or she may be congratulated for being enterprising. Parents, accustomed to people looking out for themselves, may not take a close enough look to notice that the teenager insisted on charging full price from an elderly neighbor who was on a fixed income.

This blindness to some kinds of selfishness means that teenagers' natural narcissism is reinforced, making it difficult for them to mature. As a result, they are almost totally unprepared for the real world and may balk at taking on responsibility.

But before we delve into the problems caused by teenagers' narcissism and the struggle to outgrow it, let's look at where that narcissism comes from in the first place.

NARCISSISM COMES NATURALLY

Narcissism is part of children's basic survival gear. When they are little, they see everything and everyone as extensions of themselves. It is the first step toward building their sense of self, their ego.

Children's narcissism begins with a bonding with their mothers. Children under the age of two do not differentiate between mother and self. They feel that mother is an extension of them and that they (and mother) are the core of the universe. If the mother responds to all the baby's cueing and learns the baby's personality and needs, the child feels safe and loved—the king of the world. This natural narcissism is how the child develops a sense of self and it is necessary if the child is to develop a healthy and secure identity.

By age two, however, reality begins to set in. Typically this is brought about by a parent who says, "Whoa—this kid is never going to make it in the world thinking like that. He or she has to learn some rules for getting along with people." The parent influences the child to be less emotional and less unrealistic and more logical and goal-oriented about the real world.

The Terrible Twos

The conflict betweeen child as "king" and child as "commoner" leads to the terrible conflicts that all parents dread: The child has developed this wonderful narcissistic ego on which to build a life, and then suddenly has to face the real world. The child wants to take off her clothes in the street, but her parents say, "No," and the real world intrudes on the child's mind. The child wants to eat what he wants, but his parents insist on nutritious food. Again the real world intrudes. The child tries to insist that she'll decide when she's ready to lie down and take a nap. The child uses the toilet when and where he chooses. Each time parents insist that the child will not decide, the real world conflicts with the child's narcissism.

As the child gropes with these new experiences in the real world, he or she tries to keep control. For those observing, it may seem that the child has become a tyrant. When the parents set rules, the child is outraged and throws a tantrum. The child demands that the real world conform to his or her self-centered concept. The parents cringe and worry about what they might have done wrong.

These demands and rebuffs during the terrible twos are when children make a major separation from their mothers and when they first really begin to explore and understand that outside world. It is their first experience of not being at the center of the universe and when they start to realize that they can't have it all their way.

Growing Up with Narcissism

The healthy narcissism of the infant slowly changes as the child explores the real world and comes to realize, slowly, that it does not center around him or her.

At age seven children typically take a quantum leap. They begin to realize for the first time that other people can think and feel, too. Until then, the world has been all things, objects. The presence of a pet, such as a dog or cat that can think and feel, although in an animal way, often helps the child to reach this plateau in overcoming narcissism.

Noted child development theorist Jean Piaget said that at age eleven, children develop their abstract mind. For the first time they begin thinking more as adults, planning and making decisions based on experience. Having the ability to generalize from one experience to another, they no longer see each new experience as unique. They become less self-centered and enter the final stages of development when society expects them to become as mature as adults—the teenage years.

In a very real sense, the teen years are the final extension of the terrible twos. The teenager must complete that separation from parents that began at age two. She or he still has the remains of the two-year-old's narcissism, but is now being asked to make adult decisions. In the same way that the two-year-old must face the reality that the world doesn't revolve around him, the teenager who's been provided for and protected all her life faces decisions about college and career, the responsibilities of a part-time job or driving a car, pressures to drink and do drugs, the duties of caring for younger siblings and decisions about how to handle her emerging sexual feelings. Throughout all this, teenagers have to break away and develop their own methods of handling problems, must push away from parents and their ways of doing things to establish their own adult identities.

Is it any wonder, then, that the teen years can be horrendous for parents and for teenagers themselves? How many of us would choose to relive those years?

A FEW WORDS OF HOPE AND CAUTION

Before we press on to how narcissism affects teenage behavior, for those parents who are in the midst of dealing with it, a word of hope. Typically, "bad" teenage behavior burns out between the ages of eighteen (if you're lucky) and twenty-two (if you're not). At that time, suddenly the child does in fact become an adult. The silly, selfish behavior of the teens gets put behind and the child blossoms into surprising altruism. He or she is anxious to help other people and, occasionally, even his or her parents!

One other point is worth making before we continue. As we've said, it's important to understand that narcissism is a natural part of children's normal and healthy development, but you should also know about pathological narcissism, an illness some adults suffer from. It occurs when there is no bonding, no loving mother or caretaker with whom the child can identify. This kind of narcissism requires psychological help.

Without bonding with a loving caretaker, a child has no secure basis for exploring the real world and becoming independent and mature. Without the caretaker to rely on and return to, the child can become very insecure. Ultimately, he or she may never outgrow the self-centered stage and may become pathologically narcissistic, always looking for something outside of self to make him or her feel okay.

A pathologically narcissistic adult is one who is extremely egocentric, who demands constant attention, yet who is hollow and empty within. We are *not* talking about pathological narcissism here.

With these points in mind, let's take a look at how narcissism contributes to making the teen years so traumatic and what you can do about it.

PARENTS AS PROVIDERS

One of the most common ways that teens' narcissism can cause problems is their demand for money. Teenagers tend to see their parents as providers, or "pocketbooks," rather than people with feelings.

This leads to confrontations when parents can't or won't provide what the teenager wants. Narcissistic teenagers are angry when they can't have a car because their parents can't afford it. They are outraged if their allowance has to be reduced because the family income has gone down, or if the parents expect them to start earning some money on their own.

Never having had to work a forty-hour week to support someone, they don't understand their parents' budget limitations. When parents have to pull back, the kids can't see their point of view. Kids don't care if their little brother doesn't get a bike to go to school as long as they get the car keys.

TAKING ON RESPONSIBILITY

Another place where narcissism is evident is in teens' handling of responsibility. When teens suddenly are asked to take on adult responsibilities, they usually see only how a given situation affects *them*. Thus, they often act thoughtlessly, without thinking through the results, and expect their parents to bail them out when things go wrong.

When parents can't (or won't) take care of everything, teenagers are often confused and angry. They seem amazed that things could go wrong:

"It's not fair. They had no right to fire me. They should've explained what I was doing wrong, not thrown me out!"

"I can't believe I actually had an accident with the car. It couldn't happen to me!"

"I should've been homecoming queen (or cheerleader, or football star). They had to give it to me. Mom, do something!"

BLAMING THE PARENTS

When teens suddenly find they can't control the real world, they get frustrated and angry. Their narcissism prevents them from examining themselves as a source of their problems. So they turn upon the people most susceptible to feeling guilty about their problems—their parents.

Narcissistic children often blame their parents for everything that goes wrong for them. They are hostile and sometimes even physically abusive. They use bad language, speak loudly, and do almost anything from leaving clothes lying around to outright acts of damage that they know will hurt their parents.

It is many times calculated on their part, whether consciously or unconsciously. Teenagers act the way they do because they know they can get away with it. They know you love them and are trying to understand them. Many times they are simply taking advantage of this love.

If you doubt this, consider how teenagers act with their peers. They are loving and altruistic with their friends. They want their peers to like them because deep down inside they know that this is their future (mom and dad represent the past).

A teenager very seldom gets angry or hostile to a peer. If he or she does, the peer might say, "drop dead" and leave. But that same teenager knows Mom and Dad are always going to be there, so any behavior will be okay with them.

WHAT CAN YOU DO?

If this all sounds familiar to you, if perhaps for the first time you are seeing your children in a different light, the question you're probably asking yourself is, "What can I do?"

Understanding what children are really like is the key. Once you've given up the unrealistic notion of children discussed in the introduction, you can accept that a child is naturally selfish. When you understand what's really going on, you'll find that you are less defensive. As you become aware that the child has some influence on his or her environment and may only want his or her way, you can begin to act effectively.

The Importance of Painful Experiences

To understand the child's self-centered nature and learn how to handle it, it's important to always remember that children have not had the experiences that adults have had. Their experiences in the world are limited. In large part, the process of growing up is having those experiences. This lack of experience makes it difficult for teens to understand how their actions affect others and to anticipate the results of their behavior.

Is it any surprise, then, that when children become teenagers, there is suddenly chaos? The teens suddenly are expected to start making adult decisions, but their entire life experience includes almost no encounters with pain.

"Don't you know you can kill someone by driving carelessly?" a father screams in outrage when he discovers his daughter has been speeding or acting recklessly. But, what do most teens know of death or injury? They feel immortal, immune.

"Get good grades or you won't make it to college. If you don't get to college, how will you earn a good living?" a mother warns. But has the teen seen poverty? Does he know the value, in economic terms, of an education from first-hand experiences? Again, teens who haven't seen suffering feel their lifestyle will continue on as it always has for them, regardless of what they do.

"Don't take drugs, don't have promiscuous sex!" parents plead. But have the teens had *personal* experience with the consequences of such actions? Have they seen the addict who at twenty-five looks decades older and struggles to steal enough for a fix? Have they witnessed unwed parents dealing with an unwanted child? Or what life could be like for that child?

Protecting Children from Pain

Loving parents don't want their children to experience too much pain. Therefore, they are constantly trying to guard their children from pain. The trouble is that in the process, they very often forget that pain is a normal part of living. They deprive their children of *normal pain* and life experiences.

For example, a toddler goes out to play and all the playmates are older and they don't want to play with the child. If she comes back crying, a loving parent may try to compensate by spending the rest of the day playing with the toddler.

Playing with the child is fine, but it might make her more dependent on the parent. It might feed the child's narcissism by teaching her that if things don't work out in the world, Mom and Dad will take care of her and entertain her. The lesson becomes, "Not to worry. You do not have to learn to socialize; Mom and Dad will make you feel okay."

As children experience loving parents always being there for them, what happens is the children misjudge. They think that this is the way the rest of the world is. When they eventually encounter the real world, however, they can be in for a real shock. No one else out there cares for them like their parents.

If loving parents continue to protect their children from normal pain throughout their development, they may become emotionally handicapped.

For example, a loving parent might discover that the child in junior high school has one poor teacher out of five different teachers he sees each day. To protect the child and help his education, the parent intervenes and has him moved out of that teacher's class.

However, if the child had stayed in what might have been one bad class out of five where he might not have done so well, he might have learned something invaluable—that not all teachers are good or that information isn't always going to be spoon-fed, that sometimes you need to exert great effort to get the information to succeed.

Loving parents tend to sit down with their children to carefully explain things every time there is some sort of difficult event. Given the narcissistic nature of children, it's only natural that from this, every time a difficult situation occurs, the child expects to be singled out for special treatment. As a result the child may resent the teacher who doesn't immediately stop the class to answer his or her question.

Such children have a great deal of trouble functioning as teenagers. When they get their first jobs, they are astonished when the employer doesn't kindly sit them down and tell them what they did wrong and how they can do better, but instead fires them!

They can't believe it when the school official doesn't sympathetically say, "Gee, you were late today, but I understand you had a flat tire, so we'll just let you off."

They don't know why the police officer doesn't understand and says, "I can't help it that you don't have the money to pay a ticket. Your tail lights are out."

They have come to expect one kind of treatment, and instead the world dishes out another. To them it just isn't fair.

The loving parent, by being so caring, has prevented the normal pain that would have allowed the child to mature.

HELPING TEENS OUTGROW NARCISSISM

These parents have loved too much without realizing the consequences. It's an easy trap to fall into, because the choices are tough: Do you really want to give your children negative experiences? How do you give them "learning about life" experiences? Do you sell your house and move into a dangerous neighborhood? Do you make them get a job and pay for their clothes instead of using their time to work on grades, sports, and school activities? There are no easy answers here.

The protectiveness feeds the children's narcissism. The children, in turn, become increasingly self-centered. They make ever more demands on their parents and they become increasingly intolerable (because as they face the real world, they become increasingly scared).

Ideally, parents' understanding of how pain helps children mature should dawn on them when the children are infants. If it does, then they can force themselves to allow them to experience natural pain along the way.

If children experience some pain all along, then by the time they become teenagers they will already know what the real world is like. Their narcissism will still be there, of course, but it will be tempered by reality. In many other cultures where children are less pampered, there is no teenage crisis such as there is in ours. Instead, there is a natural transition to adulthood.

The trouble is that few parents understand these concepts until it seems almost too late, until the children are already teenagers. Quite unexpectedly they are confronted by a selfish child. Caught in the middle of the whole process, what is a parent to do?

The answer, of course, is to allow the child to feel some pain, to bring reality and the child together, hopefully in a controlled and safe way. The first step, however, is to recognize when the child's behavior is narcissistic.

DON'T BLAME YOURSELF

Before we move on, keep one important concept in mind. It's important to understand that loving parents are working from their best intentions and their own childhood experiences; for that they can't be blamed. They just remember the pains of their own childhood and are trying to smooth things out for their children.

When parents have difficulty with children because they have loved too much, they often feel guilt. "It's my fault poor John (or Shirley) feels so bad."

That's a mistake. We must remember that the whole process of raising children is extremely complex and difficult. It's sort of like driving a car while looking in the mirror. You want to go left, but you have to turn the wheel right. Sometimes you have to do the opposite of what your heart tells you to do.

Remember, you don't control the situation. You share control with the child. You both have the responsibility for making it come out okay. If it doesn't, remember that it usually takes two to make a problem.

All that can be expected is that you do your best. If you do, and things come out badly, try to see the positive part that you have played. Admit that perhaps you are raising a difficult child and anyone, not just you, would have a struggle. Stop kicking yourself; it may not all be your fault.

2

Bad Personality Fits

All children have unique personalities. That's what makes Johnny distinguishable from his brother Freddy as much as their different appearances. But while most parents readily accept the notion that their children are different from each other, they don't always recognize just what an effect the child's personality type has on their relationship and on the child's development in general.

What's worse, parents often ignore another crucial fact: Sometimes a parent and a child have personalities that just don't match up very well. A very talkative and outgoing parent may have a child who is quiet and shy. Or a parent who is nervous and doesn't like to take chances may have a teen who's bold and daring. When the two have trouble getting along, the parent often feels bad and takes the blame for their problems—instead of recognizing their differences and finding ways to accommodate and even enjoy them.

RECOGNIZING A BAD FIT

The first step in finding out whether or not a "bad fit" is to blame for difficulties with your teen is to make sure you really know your child's personality traits. Although most parents recognize different personalities in other parents' children easily enough, they don't always have a good idea of exactly what traits their own children have.

A good way to recognize traits in your own children is to think of personality in terms of styles of behavior. It is possible to identify the style of your children quite easily. Very likely you already know it intuitively. For example, consider Dr. deGarcia's own family.

Heather, the first child, weighed seven pounds at birth. She was beautiful and healthy, an easy delivery. She did not want to suckle; she had to be continually awakened to eat—even coerced. Her cheeks had to be patted to get her attention. She really did not want to be held closely from day one. Today, she is still very independent and assertive—an individual with no weight problem. She can be identified by her style as easily as her appearance.

Dr. deGarcia's second daughter, Heidi, was nine pounds, also an easy birth. She came out of the womb hungry. She ate anything that stood still long enough for her to get hold of. She wanted to be nursed, cuddled, and loved continually. She would eat twenty-five hours a day if allowed. Today she is lovable, not as assertive as her sister, and continually watches her weight.

Two children, two different personality styles—yet the same parents, same environment. Parents can identify their children by their styles as easily as by their faces.

In 1956 two researchers, Alexander Thomas and Stellar Chess, compiled the New York Longitudinal Study in which they named specific traits that make up personality styles. By answering questions about these traits, you may come to see how different each of your children may be:

YOUR CHILD'S ENERGY LEVEL

Is it high, low, or medium? How does this fit in with your family style?

YOUR CHILD'S INNER TIME CLOCK

Does your child have a regular sleeping schedule and eating schedule? Can you get your child into a routine or do you find the child has a mind of his or her own and is not going to follow a pattern?

YOUR CHILD'S ABILITY TO BE FLEXIBLE AND FIT IN

Can you take your child to new places and new environments and have him or her fit right in? Or is your child uncomfortable around strangers? Do you feel nervous when you are with your child in new places or with strangers?

YOUR CHILD'S EMOTIONAL RANGE

Does your child cry too much or laugh too much? Do you find that his or her reaction to a stimulus is frequently too intense? Not intense at all? When you smile, does your child smile right back?

YOUR CHILD'S ABILITY TO ATTEND

How long is your child's attention span? Do you have to entertain her constantly or can she get involved in activities to keep herself occupied? When your child becomes involved with drawing or reading, can he sit there for hours, or is his attention span and persistence limited to only a few minutes?

These are a few traits to look at to see who your child is and what causes differences between brothers and sisters and all other children. Try identifying the personality styles of your children. Once you get started you'll be amazed. Suddenly you'll be seeing them in a whole new light. They will be individuals, not appendages of yourself.

Once you accept the fact that children have different styles and personalities that are exclusively theirs, then you're ready to tackle the guilt that can come when parent and child have different styles.

TYPES OF BAD FITS

Very often emotional explosions that seem to occur most frequently during teenage years are caused because there is a bad fit of styles between parent and child.

Ideally we would all like to be "perfect fits" with our children; we would like our personality and that of our child to be completely compatible. But far more often children have personalities that do *not* fit in every respect, or, in some cases, in hardly any respect. It's like two gears with different size teeth grinding against each other. Instead of turning smoothly together, they just clash and cause stress.

Bad fits can occur in a variety of ways:

1. EXPECTATIONS. The child may be different from what the parent was expecting. A very bright parent was expecting a bright child who would go on to college. But the child is only of average intelligence. So the parent keeps pushing the child, innocently unaware that the child is not scholastically capable. The child gets increasingly frustrated as he is not able to live up to the parent's expectations.

2. PERSONALITY STYLES. The child has a different style than the parent. The child is laid-back, quiet, not that concerned about her surroundings. The parent is nervous, on-the-go, constantly changing things. The child wants quiet time with her parent, just watching TV and talking, but the parent can't sit still that long. The parent wants to spend all day shopping, but the child gets tired after two hours. Both are continually frustrated.

3. FINANCES. Money can create bad fits. For example, a small apartment could be quite okay for an easy-going child. But it could be enormous pressure on a hyperactive one.

4. BIOLOGY. Perhaps you have an allergic child . . . and you live on a wheat farm. The allergies may cause him to be irritable, sleepless, nonsocial, withdrawn, or even aggressive.

In all of the above circumstances you can easily see that fit is critical. If parents are lucky enough to have children whose styles fit theirs, then they'll have a relatively stress-free parenting experience. On the other hand, if they have bad fits, then there can be stress and confrontations and, worst of all, self-blame.

When a bad fit happens, call it stress, a predicament, a difficult situation, or a challenge. But never, never blame. Don't blame the child and certainly don't blame yourself. Blame and the resulting guilt are inappropriate and self-defeating.

Letting go of the guilt and recognizing that this could be just a case of a bad fit can often take an enormous amount of stress out of the relationship.

GOING FORWARD

Remember, when dealing with a child, teenager, or preadolescent, you're not dealing with a mirror image of yourself.

You're not dealing with a piece of clay that you have molded and that suddenly, inexplicably, has turned into something quite different than you had in mind.

Of course it's not that easy to hang up your guilt, but if you remember that change begins with an awareness of what you are doing and how it affects you both positively and negatively, then you can begin. If you remember that you're not in the problem alone but share it with your child, then it's a little easier to avoid blaming yourself.

Remember that you're dealing with a defined, unique individual who is as intent on controlling his or her environment (perhaps more so) than you are. In other words, you're dealing with a complete human being.

When you realize this, you can accept your child's personality and start looking for some common ground. Instead of constantly pushing a studious child to be more athletic, you'll be able to value his intelligence. If you're worried that he doesn't get enough exercise, you may be able to solve the problem by realizing that he prefers solitary activities like swimming or jogging instead of the softball team you've been pushing him to join.

And if there are areas where you simply can't find common ground, you can come to accept your differences. If you're easy-going and your teen's full of energy, learn to lock yourself in your room to steal away a few quiet moments and insist that she honor those times.

With a little work, you'll find that whether or not you and your teen are a perfect fit, your lives together don't have to be a perfect mess.

3

Biology

"It's all in their jeans!"

—Erma Bombeck

We've all been taught that by creating a good home environment, by adding love in liberal doses, and by just caring, we will produce wonderful children.

But as we've already seen, that theory discounts two very important factors that can help determine how a child turns out: the child's natural narcissism and the possibility that the child's personality simply doesn't fit well with the parent's.

A third factor that is very often overlooked is the biological influence. While not nearly as common as narcissism, biological or physical problems can be at the root of many teenage difficulties. When not diagnosed and treated correctly, children can suffer from alcoholism, depression, and other seemingly psychological problems. When the problem is physical, psychological counseling won't help the child and, all too often, the parents are left with no other explanation than that they were somehow poor parents.

So let's take a look at the biological influence on two teenagers' lives to learn more about how it can affect teens and their parents.

Ann

Roger and Shirley tried to have a child of their own for several years, but were unsuccessful. They were told that their chances of having a child were one in a million. So they adopted a baby, Ann.

Two years later, Shirley got pregnant and their daughter, Leia, was born.

For Roger and Shirley it was the best of all possible worlds. They had two lovely children, a wonderful family. What could possibly go wrong?

For the first fourteen years of Ann's life, everything seemed fine. She was tested as a bright girl, although she did not do particularly well in school. She didn't do badly, she just never excelled. Leia, on the other hand, did not test high, but worked very hard and got better grades than her sister.

Shirley, who was a strict parent, insisted that the older girl do better. Roger, who was more lenient, kept saying, "Don't push her, Shirley. She's doing the best she can." Roger was continually buying presents for the children and Shirley was continually saying to him, "You'll spoil them."

When the Real Trouble Started

By the time Ann was fifteen, Roger and Shirley were having trouble with her. They both worked and she refused to stay home after school.

They would come home from work and she wouldn't be there, not coming home until after dark.

They tried everything to restrict her, but all to no avail. She stopped doing any chores, her grades got much worse at school, and she began using terrible language around the house.

Roger and Shirley were at wit's end. They insisted that Ann go with them to see a counselor.

But Ann's behavior deteriorated. Once she stayed out all night and acted surprised when Roger and Shirley told her they'd spent the night calling her school, the police, and the hospitals in a panic. She began cutting classes, lying, and refusing to do her chores.

Then Ann ran away. After three and a half weeks, Roger and Shirley found her living with three other teenagers in a rented apartment, haggard and hungry, sleeping on the floor.

Roger and Shirley checked Ann into a psychiatric hospital to find out what was wrong. At the doctor's advice, they ignored her pleas to come home.

Within a week Ann escaped. This time it took Roger and Shirley over a month to track her down in another city thirty-five miles away.

This time they took her home. They said they would do anything to work things out. Ann's demands were simple: no more school, no more restrictions of any kind. She would stay at home if her parents were simply providers. Else, she was gone.

Roger and Shirley tried. But within a week they discovered they could not live that way. Ann would come and go at any time of the day or night. She would have friends over. They would play loud records and mess up the kitchen. It was intolerable. They could not have a child acting like a tyrant in their home.

Finally Roger and Shirley laid down the law. Ann could live there *if* she followed prescribed rules. On the other hand, if she ran away again, they would not search to find her. In fact, they would not allow her to return unless she signed a contract agreeing to their demands. (Tough Love, the organization that deals with difficult teenage children, was helping them now.)

But the pattern continued. Ann ran away again, then came home and signed the agreement. She went back to school, but began drinking heavily. She ran away with a boyfriend and disappeared for a year. An alcohol detoxification center called to say Ann was there, but by the time they arrived Ann had already left. They heard bits and pieces about her over the next few years, but did not have any solid contacts.

Their natural daughter, Leia, on the other hand, was a more typical teenager. She went through a period of adjusting her perspective to the world. She was angry when the universe did not correspond to her narcissistic views. She threw some two-year-old-type tantrums, submitted to peer pressure and wore her hair in a weird style, and sometimes growled instead of talked.

However, she never ran away, never did badly in school (though the work was hard for her), and by the time she was seventeen had matured into a fine, altruistic young woman her parents were proud of.

ENVIRONMENT OR HEREDITY?

What happened with Ann? Why did Leia turn out one way and Ann another?

Shirley and Roger were guilt-ridden. They blamed themselves for what had happened. Shirley felt she had been too strict with the older girl. Roger felt he had been too lenient. A therapist told them that the combination of different parenting styles had led to the problems with Ann. In other words, they were to blame.

But Shirley could not accept that. It just didn't sit well with her. They had used the same parenting styles with Leia and she had turned out so wonderfully. So Shirley spent nearly a year tracking down Ann's natural parents. She discovered that Ann's natural mother had been an alcoholic. Her natural father had been a drifter, never settling down.

It turned out that Ann's lifestyle as a young adult mirrored her natural parents'. It was totally foreign to her adopted parents.

But even after Shirley met Ann's natural mother, she could not escape her guilty feelings. The therapist insisted that children are the products of the parents with whom they live, not their natural parents. When Shirley came in to see Dr. deGarcia, she was still trying to figure out exactly what she had done wrong.

Shirley and Roger eventually came to realize they were not to blame. Genetics and biology both play their role in a child's development. They were loving parents who did the best they could, but just ended up with a bad biological fit.

Blaming Roger and Shirley was not only wrong, it was cruel. Perhaps, if Shirley and Roger had recognized the importance of the biological influence, they might have done some things differently. But feeling guilty that they had somehow failed Ann only added to their pain.

What could Roger and Shirley have done had they known? The biological influence is strong. But sometimes it can be countered. Although Ann's actions may have originated in her genes, the immediate cause may have been chemical imbalances in her body. If Roger and Shirley had been given advice to have Ann checked for vitamin deficiencies and allergies, they might have been helped. Avoiding certain foods and taking certain supplements might have stabilized her emotions and reduced her susceptibility to addictive substances.

If they were aware of the potential in her genes, Roger and Shirley might also have noted the behavioral patterns earlier and sought therapy sooner. Perhaps they could have found a hobby for her in order to keep her very busy and allow her to excel in areas in which she had innate skills.

Sometimes, as the above story illustrates, a child's biological makeup can be every bit as important as the environment in which she is raised. Even natural brothers and sisters may react differently to the same situations.

Tuning in to the fact that there may be some biological factors influencing a child can lead to a happier resolution. Of course, that means giving up the preconceived notion that parents are to blame for everything their children do.

Jose

Jose was an 18-year-old getting ready to graduate from high school. However, when he came in to see Dr. deGarcia, his graduation was in doubt, as was his entire future. He was suffering from alcoholism, depression, severe anxiety, and panic attacks (moments when he would lose control fearing some imaginary threat).

He walked with a kind of despairing gloom. Although he should have just been starting life, he was instead seeing it as a short corridor leading down. He had a long face, a slow gait, and he dressed roughly.

Worst of all, he had been in trouble with the police and was now facing his second count for drunk driving.

Jose's natural parents were loving, caring people. Neither of them drank. They both held responsible jobs and were immensely concerned about Jose.

They loved their son, but no matter what they did, his personality seemed to deteriorate and his behavior grew worse. He began drinking at thirteen and they had not been able to get him to stop.

Eventually they took him to an alcoholic rehabilitation center, but even this produced no lasting results. They worked with him for years, all to no avail. For some reason he simply did not respond.

Through medical doctors at the rehabilitation hospital, Jose was put on a drug that inhibited his alcoholism. This "anti-abuse" drug made him sick whenever he would drink alcohol.

Jose seemed sincerely interested in helping himself and he strictly adhered to the treatment. He took the drug and very soon he was completely off alcohol.

However, that only made the rest of his condition worse. He began to have severe depression. His weight dropped by nearly thirty pounds. At the end of three months he began to have regular panic attacks. As a result, he could not stand to be around other people or in any kind of stressful situation.

Jose would break out in a sweat just going into a restaurant. He would become fearful and have to leave grocery lines. He had a very difficult time controlling himself while driving on the freeway.

At this time he was placed on an anti-depressant. Immediately, he began to feel better. Within a few weeks the panic attacks stopped, as did his general anxiety. Suddenly, he found he could fully function in society. He could be in a classroom with a large group of people without his heart pounding. He could drive on the freeways, stand in lines—do all the things that he could not do before . . . and do them with ease.

His outlook brightened. All at once his dark future seemed much lighter. He was taken off the anti-alcoholic abuse drug, yet he did not return to drinking. He had lost the need and craving for alcohol. He did graduate and then entered a junior college where he did very well.

Jose's parents were overjoyed. They said they hadn't seen him so happy since before he was a teenager. He seemed to be a new person. It was as if their beloved son had been lost for half a dozen years and was now miraculously returned to them.

A BIOLOGICAL CAUSE

Jose had a physical problem called biodepression (biological depression). He was always depressed, but the cause was in his physical makeup. This led to all of his other symptoms, including alcoholism. The condition had manifested itself when he reached adolescence.

Prior treatments, attempting to handle the matter psychologically, had failed because they did not get at the root of the problem. It had been like trying to treat a broken leg with psychoanalysis. It was only when the biological problem was addressed that a cure was found.

Jose, his family, and his friends suffered for years because the false assumption was made that his actions were a result of the environment his parents had created for him. They had taken Jose in for counseling and had been told that their parenting was the problem. They had explained that Jose's problems had started when he became a teenager and the counselor had immediately told them that they allowed things to get out of hand. They tried to explain that they had done all they could, but the therapist continued to blame them. The truth was that no matter what Jose's parents might have done, the results would have been virtually the same.

Metabolically, not all of us have a fully functioning endocrine system. For some children, the problem truly is in the glands. It might be biodepression, as was the case here. Or it might be allergies or something else. But when a child acts "crazy" it's important *not* to first blame the parents.

Instead, a good physical including allergy and blood testing may prove more beneficial.

HOW BIOLOGICAL IS IT?

The tendency, after reading a chapter such as this, is to say, "It's all biological." After all, we've just had two rather dramatic examples where the emotional problems of the child were probably physical in origin.

It's important to note, however, that while there may be a biological cause, in *most* cases, there is not. In most cases the problem is psychological in nature.

So it's important not to first jump to the conclusion that difficult behavior is biologically induced. If you suspect that it is, some medical testing may be in order. But even so, don't anticipate that you'll always get a quick fix with some miracle drugs. Far more likely, it will take concentrated effort on the parents' part with the help of doctors, nutritionists, therapists, and medication to turn the child around.

What's critical is for parents not to be overcome by feelings of guilt for things beyond their control. It's no more the parents' fault that their child has an endocrine problem than that he is narcissistic or has a personality that does not fit well with theirs.

4
Peer Pressure

Parents of teenagers know all about peer pressure. Kids sometimes seem like cows in a herd. They all want to act, look, even think the same way. Should anyone show any individuality, the peers shun that person until he or she falls back into line. Peer pressure rules the teenager.

The basic reason for this is that teens instinctively know that the future lies with their peers. The family is the past. Therefore, getting along with the others is akin to survival.

For parents, this can be overwhelming. The teenager treats parents like second-class citizens. Everything is done for peers.

Parents can see that they're losing control. Seemingly all at once the teenager stops responding to their wishes and instead responds to the wishes of peers. Parents are worried by this loss of control.

THE PERVASIVENESS OF PEER PRESSURE

If you doubt the importance of peer pressure during the teen years, consider those teens who are admiringly looked upon as rebels by their friends. Perhaps it is the color or style of their hair or their clothing that sets them apart. But the teens know who the rebels are—just ask anyone.

Then look at those rebels more closely. All the rebels look alike! In fact, there are two major groups of teenagers—those who conform to the majority and those who conform to the minority (the rebels). But they all *conform* to those whom they consider their peers. The truth is there are no (or at least very few) true teenage nonconformists. Such is the power of peer pressure.

IT STARTS VERY EARLY

What most people fail to see is that the teenager who responds to peer pressure is different only by degree from the five-year-old who also responds to peer pressure. To put it another way, all children who socialize respond to the pressure of their peers. Teenagers just do it more intensely.

At earlier ages peer pressure is also there. However, the parents are so powerful that children are forced to conceal that response. It's only when they become teenagers and begin to acquire the power of adults that they are able to reveal how they feel about pressure from their peers.

It isn't that parents suddenly lose their children to their friends when they become teenagers. It's that they suddenly realize how influential those friends have always been. Teen peer pressure isn't so much anything new to the child as it is a new realization for the parent.

To get an idea of how important a factor peer pressure is early on in a child's life, consider the case of Steve.

Steve

Jack and Marie carefully planned their child's birth and were delighted to have a laughing, happy, chubby son they named Steve.

They reared him with love and consideration and tried their very best to impart good values. Then, when he was five years old, they sent Steve off to kindergarten, his first real opportunity at socialization.

But by the middle of the year, Steve had become a "problem." He was lying about everything both at school and to Jack and Marie. At school he was harrassing the teacher. Along with a couple of other children, he was laughing and giggling and disrupting the class. One day he came home with a crude tattoo on his arm made with a ballpoint pen and a needle.

Trying to Get Support from the School

Jack and Marie called for a parent conference. They wanted to find out what was going on and correct it. Steve had been a wonderful little boy until he started school. Since then his behavior had badly deteriorated. What had happened at school?

The teacher told them it was just a stage that Steve was passing through. He'd outgrow it. After all, it was just kindergarten. She suggested that they "lighten up . . . Cut your son some slack and he'll come around."

Jack and Marie immediately felt guilt. They listened to the teacher and looked into themselves for the fault. All along, they now believed, they had been harming their child by being too strict. They vowed to change, to ease up. They anticipated Steve's behavior would then improve.

Instead, his behavior grew steadily worse. Finally Marie, desperate, decided to investigate by herself. With the permission of the teacher, she attended several days' worth of classes.

She discovered that Steve had befriended two other children. He sought them out as his regular playmates and he was obviously influenced by them.

Going to the houses of the other parents, purportedly to bring Steve over to play, Marie found that the families were extremely loose with their children. They enforced little or no discipline. They let the kids do what they wanted, dress as they wanted, and, essentially, act as if they controlled their own lives (as adults do).

These other children were very different from what Steve had been used to. Steve, of course, was very naive and innocent coming from a fairly healthy family. When he discovered these other two boys he was fascinated by them. These boys did things he considered exciting, risky. To Steve, they were more attractive than normal, comfortable, mentally healthy and stable children. So he emulated them.

These children didn't respond in school the way the other children did. They would talk back to the teacher, act and laugh out of turn, and were generally disrespectful. Steve mimicked their behavior.

The bottom line was that Steve was not going through a stage at all. He was not "mentally ill" as his mother had feared nor a "discipline problem" as his father had suggested. He was simply responding to peer pressure.

Once Marie and Jack realized this, they cleared up the situation almost immediately. They moved Steve to another school. Steve no longer saw his friends. In the new school's environment, there were no other children who acted as his former friends did.

Without the peers to support his former behavior, Steve changed. He became the respectful, friendly, happy boy he had been before.

THE LESSON OF PEER PRESSURE

Jack and Marie had blamed themselves needlessly. They realized that they had punished themselves for problems they hadn't caused. They simply didn't take into account the influence of outsiders, most specifically, peers. Until Marie actually investigated and saw for herself what was happening, it never dawned on either of them that a child of five could be so influenced by other children. If Jack and Marie hadn't assumed the blame for their son's behavior and hadn't stopped their investigation so soon, they could have solved the problem much more quickly.

The lesson here is one that should be taken to heart by all parents whether their children are five or fifteen. A lot of what happens, a great deal of what your child does or does not do is determined not by you, but by your child's friends. Peer pressure at any age of socialization is enormous. Even at five it can be *stronger than the influence of the parent in certain areas!* If that's the case, just imagine how strong it is when the child is a teenager.

WHAT TO DO?

In the case of Steve the solution was fairly obvious and easy. Change schools. Remove the peers and the problem would dissolve.

However, as children grow older, this solution becomes less of an option. The children become more mobile. They can ride their bikes over to the houses of friends who live great distances away. Restricting them becomes more difficult.

Moving the family out of the area—which can be a solution in some cases—also gets more difficult as children get older. It also may not be a possibility because of financial considerations. You may simply not be able to afford to move for the sake of the kids.

If you can't simply isolate your children from peers who are having a bad influence on them, what can you do?

The first thing to do is to realize the magnitude of the problem. The pressure of peers can be greater than the parents' influence.

Second, you can forbid your children to be with certain other teens and mean it. As parents, you still have some influence and kids sometimes will do what you want. If you carefully explain that your child is not to associate with a friend or there will be dire consequences (that you back up), you may find your wishes respected. This alone may be enough to cure the problem.

Of course, the teenager might rebel against this and not comply, but many times parents need to make a stand. If your teen chooses to sneak and do it anyway, you may not always be able to prevent it. But the teen will definitely know where you stand on this issue. Remember, you may not always be loved for what you do, but that is okay. It is better to stand up for what you believe than to let a teen do something that you know will be harmful.

Third, there is the matter of explaining to your children just what it is you object to in a particular peer. But beware of this. The very things you object to may be what your child admires. This may particularly be the case if you run a "tight ship" and the other child comes from a family that is loose.

In a case like this, time may be on your side. While your teen may at first only see the benefits of the looser family structure, over a period of time the drawbacks, such as lack of care, not as much support, and other such negative factors may appear.

Finally, you can take a positive approach and work to interest your child in other activities. Get him or her started in the school speech club or a soccer team. Dance, music, art, and computer classes are always available. As you multiply the opportunities for your child to socialize with many other teens, the appeal of one particular "bad" child is bound to diminish.

CHILDREN STEER TOWARD "EXCITING" PEERS

Remember that many times a problem child may be exciting to a normal child. There may be a bond there that is akin to someone falling in love with a terribly exciting, neurotic personality. Teenagers may somehow get addicted to another kid because the "naughtiness" is so appealing as compared to his or her normal "boring" activities.

Also naive children who have been basically protected may really not know or understand the consequences of their friends' actions. In children's narcissistic viewpoint, all people are good and caring like their parents and family. They may not realize that there are evil or mean people out there, or that their friends may have psychological problems because they have been raised in a dysfunctional family.

The naive teen may not understand the consequences until he is up to his neck in disaster in a room full of kids doing drugs or she is alone with a guy who is trying to molest her. Both may have innocently thought it was all a game until they were finally confronted or trapped in a bad situation.

TAKE ACTION

Do not be afraid to have your child get angry at you because you restricted him from a friend. Forget what people say about, "You can't keep your child from that friend. He'll sneak out and see him anyway."

So what? You'll make it really hard for that to happen. And if it does, at least your child will know that you do not condone the friendship.

So if you have a queasy feeling in your stomach about a kid your child is running with, stand up and be counted. It is better to go by your instincts and be disliked than to be sorry later when something bad happens. This is especially true if you see your child's personality change and he or she seems addicted to that friend.

If you try your best to stop it, you'll feel better about yourself than if you let your child stay in a friendship that really looks and feels bad to you.

5

Sibling Rivalry

"Mom always loved you best!"

—Tommy Smothers
of the Smothers Brothers

There is nothing that quite matches the anger of sibling rivalry. An older child, who has been king of the roost, is suddenly displaced by a new arrival. Unable to accept sharing parental attention or a diminishing of his or her role, the older child may throw angry tantrums, spill and throw food, cry, and so forth, at least until the older sibling gets used to the idea that he or she does not dominate the world.

If you have more than one child, you undoubtedly have had a taste of sibling rivalry. Maybe one child wants more attention because he is the youngest, or the sickest, or the weakest. Or maybe a younger child resents having to live up to the older's reputation in school. Whatever the situation, sibling rivalry usually comes out of children jockeying for position. Often it's caused by jealousy or a feeling that there's just not enough love and attention to go around.

Most parents treat sibling rivalry as just one more stage that they must go through with their children. But a few children never completely outgrow it. Instead, it continues to influence their behavior throughout the teen years, and shapes their relationships with their brothers and sisters in ways that will remain long after they have matured into adults.

When sibling rivalry remains intense and causes severe family problems, parents often are unaware of the source of the difficulty. They know that one child is always complaining, but the reason for the complaints isn't clear. Frequently, parents of children who have not matured past sibling rivalry blame themselves for their children's problems . . . and accept guilt for them as well.

Jennifer

Jennifer was only two when her father died. It was a difficult time, but not long afterward her mother remarried a really wonderful man. Her new father idealized Jennifer and legally adopted her.

They made a marvelous family, the three of them. Then Jennifer's parents had another child. The parents were pleased. They had such a lovely family, now it would simply be larger.

But Jennifer, who was now ten years old, simply would not accept the younger child. Until the baby had shown up, she had been number one. She had two parents all to herself.

Now their time was shared . . . and shared badly. The baby cried all the time and her parents had to spend most of their time with her. And she did all kinds of things to get the parents' attention so they would be exhausted and have no energy left for Jennifer.

Jennifer began to try to harrass and hurt the baby, and her parents had to watch her closely. Instead of tapering off slowly, as most sibling rivalry does, Jennifer's jealousy continued to grow.

Jennifer's parents tried to reason with her. They worked closely with her to help her adjust, and they consulted a pediatrician and other professionals. They asked Jennifer, "What can we do?"

Her answer was obvious: Stop spending time with the baby. Listen to my needs and desires.

The parents vowed to work even harder to make Jennifer feel loved. They went out of their way to give Jennifer more attention. But she seemed to be insatiable. No matter what they did, it was never enough. Jennifer had learned how to become the victim and even believed the role. "You always loved Cindy more than me. Everything you've ever done proved that."

Despite her parents' efforts, Jennifer never overcame her jealousy. Even as a teen, Jennifer would recall in vivid detail every mishap, wrong move, or perceived injustice. This only made the parents feel worse. If Jennifer thought this, then surely they had treated her badly. They felt as if they had actually abused Jennifer.

Starting Her Own Family

Eventually Jennifer moved out, married, and started her own family, but still her complaining continued. Cindy grew up and did well in school and socially. This only seemed to heighten Jennifer's bitterness. It was as though Jennifer were entitled to a royal crown, but somehow her parents had stolen it from her and placed it on Cindy's head.

The parents didn't want to cut Jennifer off, so they put up with the complaints and insults. And they always looked into their own actions to see if, indeed, Jennifer was right. After all, the father had adopted Jennifer, while Cindy was his natural daughter. Had he played favorites? The mother worried about this same thing and about her inadvertently going along with the playing of favorites.

Their lives were so agonized by Jennifer's continual complaints that even years after she left home, they did not feel at peace. It affected all aspects of their lives and kept them from enjoying life fully.

WAS THE RIVAL CHILD JUSTIFIED?

Was Jennifer right? Did she have a reason to complain? In truth, Jennifer was simply narcissistic. As a child, she saw the world so unrealistically that she truly believed it was there just for her pleasure. Then Cindy came along and ruptured her world view. Suddenly things didn't work out pleasantly anymore. Her parents were off tending someone else. The world no longer catered to her every whim.

Facing the reality that she was not a princess, not the center of the world, was painful for Jennifer. Rather than face it, she blamed Cindy. It was Cindy's fault that she hurt. Cindy caused it all.

But her parents protected Cindy from Jennifer's anger. It was then that Jennifer saw that it wasn't really Cindy who was at fault after all. It was her parents. They had brought Cindy into the world and they were now defending her. They were the reason that Jennifer's world was collapsing.

So Jennifer blamed her parents and punished them every chance she got. It was wonderfully convenient for her. Whenever anything went wrong with her life, she could blame her parents for having Cindy.

COPING WITH JEALOUSY

Jennifer's parents allowed themselves to be taken in by her complaining. When she felt pain at being deposed as empress of the realm, they naturally felt sorry for her pain.

But they went the one step further. They assumed blame.

They felt guilt when Jennifer felt bad. And the worse Jennifer complained and the more she blamed them, the guiltier they felt. They believed that they were indeed at fault.

If they did anything wrong, it was to accept blame. The guilt that resulted paralyzed them. It kept them from acting with purpose to diffuse Jennifer's accusations. The guilt kept them from being able to effectively help Jennifer.

While their hearts told them to give increasing amounts of attention to Jennifer (in truth, over the years she undoubtedly received far more attention than Cindy), it might have been wiser for Jennifer's parents to be absolutely equal with their attention. Rather than continue to fawn over Jennifer when she complained, they might have scrupulously divided up their time. Jennifer has a special day; Cindy has a special day. Jennifer gets a toy; Cindy gets a toy, and so forth.

This might not have changed Jennifer immediately. She probably wouldn't be happy with anything less than the total attention of her parents, so any attempt at being fair would have been rebuffed.

The people it would have helped are the parents. If they truly felt that they were giving equal attention to each child, then they could have ignored Jennifer's accusations. The advantage of being able to do this is that they would not feel guilty for Jennifer's problem. They would not adopt that problem as their own.

Not being encumbered by guilt, Jennifer's parents could have acted decisively in all areas. More important, Jennifer would have eventually seen that her accusations and complaining were falling on deaf ears. How long would she have kept it up if she saw that neither parent was paying a bit of attention to it?

Because they felt guilty, Jennifer's parents felt compelled to dote over her. This fed her narcissism. In effect, the very attention they gave her helped keep her immature.

Had they been able to gain some distance from the problem and see that answering with the heart was only making it worse, they might have effectively helped Jennifer.

This is an important lesson for all parents dealing with teenage rivalry. Sometimes it's more important to think and get the right answer than to give way to feelings. Your child may feel pain when he has to share time and attention with a brother or she feels she's being compared to her older sister, but that doesn't mean you should rush right in and try to make everything better. It might be wiser to let the child feel that pain and outgrow that green-eyed monster called sibling rivalry.

6
Working Parents

Today more than half of all American families have two breadwinners. The days when dad went off to earn the bacon and mom stayed at home to care for the kids are largely a thing of the past.

But no matter how common it is, working parents, particularly working moms, have a special cross to bear. It is a combination of guilt and accusation that comes from a society that's still adjusting to the two-breadwinner family. Even if it's boring for mom to stay at home or if the family desperately needs the money, parents who both work are made to feel that they're putting work before the child's welfare. That leads, inevitably, to guilt.

In this chapter we're going to see how kids take advantage of a working parent's guilt and just what really are the consequences of both parents working. Once we do, hopefully, working parents will begin to feel a little less guilt and will be better able to meet the challenges of managing a two-income family.

THE HURT DOE

Have you ever seen the "hurt doe" look in your child's eyes? You know the look. You've got one morning a week that you don't have to be at work by seven. You know you can sleep in until 10 o'clock and, by God, you're going to do just that!

Then a child walks in on you. He or she has to go to school or get ready to play soccer or needs a ride to the mall or wants breakfast or can't find that new blue shirt.

What are you going to do, pretend you're still asleep, pretend that you don't hear him? If you do, those innocent doe eyes will fill with tears of hurt or hate or whatever they know will ring your chimes. You really have no alternative but to get up and get what they want.

Of course, you could always say, "I'm just too tired. Do it yourself." But you never do. The reason is you feel guilty because you're not meeting their needs and desires. All children have their own special way of making a working parent feel guilty if you're too tired to make their lunch, take them to the park, play cards with them, or just talk to them.

The child's motivation is to get something, often to get the parent to stay home and cater to her or him. The child is intelligent and has ample time to study the parents, carefully investigating their buttons until he or she learns which ones to push in just the right sequence to get just the desired result. The child learns how to take full advantage of the working parent's guilt.

Greg

Gloria had a neat, close family. She had two sons, seven and ten, and she and her husband worked with the kids as a team. They met weekly for a family "clearing" time, went on family vacations, and played together nightly. Gloria and her husband were child-oriented, continually working with their children on schoolwork, special interests, hobbies, and sports.

When Gloria went back to work, therefore, it was a surprise to them that they encountered so many problems from the ten-year-old, Greg. To use his own word, Greg was "pissed" at his mom for leaving home.

Greg was in no way going to accept his mother's time being taken away from him. He liked his lunches being made for him. He liked the cookies and milk after school. Even though Gloria was going back to teaching and would be home almost the same time as Greg, he didn't like it.

Greg decided to punish his mother. He knew her very well from ten years of intensive study and he knew exactly which buttons to push.

He started by pretending to be sick in order to get Gloria to stay home with him. He would put hot water in his mouth to raise his temperature just before Gloria took it. He swallowed raw eggs in order to throw up. He complained about stomach pains. Gloria, thinking he was physically sick, did just what he wanted—she stayed home with him.

It took a while, but eventually Gloria discovered that Greg was faking. Now, however, she faced an even bigger decision. If Greg was so upset about her leaving home and going off to work that he faked illness, didn't that mean that he had a psychological problem? And if so, shouldn't she spend time caring for him? Either way, Gloria stayed home and Greg won.

When Gloria realized Greg was faking physical illness, he moved on to new territory. He read articles about children needing nurturing from mothers and brought these up with Gloria, asking her opinion. He memorized a teacher's statement about how he was now a "latch key" kid.

This almost broke Gloria's heart. Finally, she decided that she could no longer work outside the home.

Being a homemaker, however, would not work either, Gloria soon discovered. Staying at home for two children who were at school most of the time was simply boring for her. She tried to lose herself in lasagna recipes, working out in the gym, taking classes, and meeting with friends . . . all to no avail. There were just too many hours to fill and the thought of wasting precious time was intolerable to her.

Finally, she sat Greg down and told him, "It's either you go into therapy or I do. I've already paid my dues, so you'll have to do it. I'm going back to work and you're going to have to adjust to it. I love you, but get off my back!"

Needless to say, Greg didn't like it. But he had a choice of either accepting it, or continuing to throw two-year-old kinds of tantrums.

Once Greg finally realized that his game was really over, he almost instantly gave up the behaviors that had given his mother so much grief and got on with his own life.

DO IT YOURSELF

While Gloria brought Greg in to Dr. deGarcia for therapy that really wasn't essential, it was just that Gloria had no idea what was happening. She didn't realize how narcissistic Greg was. She thought the child had severe psychological problems. It wasn't until after some counseling that she realized it was simply a lack of maturation on his part.

Gloria could have simply been firm with Greg by herself without therapy. The results would undoubtedly have been similar. All it took was for Greg to realize that times had changed, that his view of the world had been wrong, and that either he had to face reality and grow up or forever remain a kid.

THROWING OFF THE CLOAK OF GUILT

For a very long time, Gloria could not act because she was paralyzed by guilt. If you're a working parent, you may feel the same way. That's terribly unfortunate since there usually is no real reason to geel guilty for working. If you would like to throw off your own guilt, consider these questions:

1. Do you realize how many parents there are in society who, just like you, continually feel guilty about working? You are not alone. *Everyone feels the same way!*

2. Do you realize that society is against you? Everyone from the evening news to teachers keeps hammering away about the problems of "latch key" kids. Of course the purported goal is to inform, but the real effect of such discussion is to make working parents feel guilty.

3. Does the fact that you work necessarily mean that your child is going to be affected *negatively?* Your going off to work may be the best thing that could happen to your child.

   Having working parents means the child will be forced to take on responsibilities. Of course, some of those responsibilities may be painful, like not having a loving, comforting, warm mom or dad waiting there when they come home from school. That's unpleasant. But it's not horrible. In life we can't expect someone to always be waiting for us.

Similarly, making his or her own lunches and cleaning up rooms are also painful in their own ways. But they are normal pains. Could it actually be *better* for your child to experience these than not?

Many studies show that there are benefits from both parents working, if adequate child care and supervision are still provided. These include having more self-reliant, less selfish, and more considerate children.

4. Do you think it's your fault if the kids seem to have problems when you go back to work?

Many parents do. But the problems could be no one's fault. Consider this from a different perspective. Let's say for a moment that instead of the problem being caused by your going back to work, it was caused by your race, religion, or ethnicity.

Many children blame their parents for race, religion, or ethnicity problems. If they feel that they don't fit in with the majority, very often they will say, "You did it!" It's their parents' fault because they are a different color or a minority religion or they come from a different ethnic background. "Mom, why couldn't you have been white, Anglo-Saxon, Protestant?"

Would you buy into such immature thinking? Certainly not. So if you won't buy into feeling guilt because of your race, religion, or ethnicity, why buy into feeling guilt because you have to or want to work? Does it make any more sense?

If your daughter comes home and says, "Mom, it's your fault because I didn't get selected for the sorority because you work and you can't drive me around," do you feel guilty? Or do you laugh?

When your son says, "Dad, the guys don't accept me because you are a plumber and their dads are all office workers," do you feel guilty? Or do you think how selfish your child is acting?

Fight back! You're not the perfect parent. No one is. That doesn't mean you're not a great parent. That doesn't mean that you should be paralyzed by guilt.

Throw off your guilt and suddenly you will see just how ridiculous many of the manipulative statements of our children really are.

"STAGE DOOR" PARENTS

Thus far we've been talking about parents who feel guilt because they must work and can't spend as much time as they'd like with their kids. There is, however, another side to this coin. Suppose you work and to compensate for this, you devote extra time to the child. Society may come down just as hard on you for being a "stage door" parent.

The stage-door syndrome occurs when caring parents are so determined that their children should not suffer because of their work that they push much harder than non-working parents. It gets its name from the story of Shirley Temple. Ms. Temple's mother reportedly took Shirley to every possible audition in the hopes of getting her a part in a play or movie. The mother would then wait anxiously at the "stage door" for the girl after the audition or show.

In this book, the term *stage door parents* means working parents who push their child into all sorts of activities because they feel guilty for not being able to spend time with that child.

Stage door parents are those who take their child to every soccer game or tennis tournament. They enroll their daughter in language classes and piano lessons and take her to every session. If you're the sort who's up in the morning chalking the line where your son will play football later in the day or selling tickets to the game and working double time in the snackbar, then you're a stage door parent, or so some will say.

But it's not necessarily bad. It can be a wise decision on your part. You may have decided that you're going to put your life on hold during those years of sports lessons and school activities so that your child will be better and brighter. The trouble is, society may knock you for it. You may be told that you're pushing your kid too hard, or that you're trying to live vicariously through the kid. You may be warned not to let your child run your life.

WHAT TO DO

When society makes you feel guilty for becoming involved with the children, you should do two things.

First ask yourself why people are saying these things and whether you really care what they say.

When you become greatly involved with the kids, very often other parents look bad by comparison. They don't like it, so they use some "common wisdom" psychology to put the involved parent down. With this kind of motivation, should you really pay attention to what they are saying?

Second, if you're concerned about what society at large and certain people in particular are thinking about you, ask yourself, "Will that other person ever be there for me or my family if we are really in a health or financial or other crisis? Will they be there to give us emotional, financial, or other support?" In other words, are they truly my friends?

For about 99 percent of the world, the answer is, "No!" And if those people you worry about are not supportive to your family, why should you care what they may say? So what if you are out there lining the field or working the soft drink stand or taking your child to dance classes or extra activities? As long as you find it fulfilling and don't push the child beyond his or her capabilities, are you doing any harm or good? If it's good, why feel guilty?

Once you realize that it's your child's welfare that you need think about, not what other people may be thinking, you can stop feeling guilty about being a stage door parent.

DAMNED BOTH WAYS

The point we're trying to make here is that it's really a no-win situation for a working parent when it comes to guilt. If you don't have the time to spend with your "latch key" child, then society beats you down for what you've done. On the other hand, if in spite of your work, you really do get involved, then people assume you're either overcompensating for work, or you're trying to live your life through your child and they say you're a stage door parent.

You can't win. You're damned if you do and damned if you don't. No matter what you do, according to society your kid is going to be screwed up *and it's going to be your fault!*

DUMPING GUILT

Guilt is the great enemy of the working parent. It gets in the way of what's good for the parent and, what's worse, it often can get in the way of what's good for the children. Guilt keeps parents from being more positive and creative and it allows children to play on that guilt to get their own way. Remember, as a working parent, you do not have as much time as you would like—do not waste it feeling guilty.

If you work and you also try as hard as you can to be a loving, caring parent, then you are to be applauded. You have chosen what may be a more difficult road, but one that may ultimately make both you and your child better people.

7
Divorce

A divorce may mean strong emotional pain for a teenager for perhaps the first time in his or her life. All of a sudden the teen is not first in the minds of the parents. The attention, the economic goodies, the easy and comfortable home life may be threatened all at once. In addition, the teen may be thrust into an environment with a stepparent he or she strongly resents.

The result can be a new experience for the teenager—loss and pain.

Rather than deal with the situation and say, "I've been hurt, but I understand that it's not my fault, it's not my parents' fault, it's just life," the teen often blames one parent, probably the most vulnerable one. Teens strike out at whoever they think caused their pain, without seeing the pain they are inflicting.

Our goal in this chapter is to understand what teens caught in the pain of divorce are capable of doing and why. Then parents can see the force they are dealing with, come to terms with their own guilt, and find the best ways to help their teens through this trauma.

THE VULNERABLE PARENT

As a divorced parent (whether taking care of your kids or stepchildren, whether single or remarried), you are very vulnerable. You are vulnerable because you love and care. You want the best for the children. When things don't go well, you feel it's your fault and guilt begins to creep in and paralyze you.

You are, literally, at your weakest when meeting one of parenting's greatest challenges. Divorced parents usually just want things to work out with their kids. They've had enough conflict and stress. They want peace and love.

Teen children, on the other hand, very rarely see clearly what the parents need. What these children see is the vulnerability of the parent. They see that they can use that vulnerability to relieve their own pain or achieve their own goals.

Stu and Kathleen

Marian thought she had the storybook family life. She married a quiet, but caring man. She was sure he loved her and was equally sure about her love for him.

They had two children whom they named Stu and Kathleen. Since her husband was a professional and made enough money to support a family, Marian didn't have to worry about working and mothering at the same time. They both agreed it would be best if she stayed home exclusively to raise the babies.

Stu and Kathleen were healthy, wonderful children. They both got good grades and were active in sports.

When the younger of these two was eight years old, Marian and her husband decided that they wanted to add to their family. They enjoyed their kids, their roles as parents, and each other. Marian said, "It seemed we had fallen into something we were really good at, so why not continue?"

They had two more children, another darling little boy and finally a girl who was the "apple of her daddy's eye." Again both children were healthy, smart, and active. Life seemed perfect.

Then, when Marian's husband was in his mid-forties, he reached a mid-life crisis. Whereas before he had enjoyed devoting himself to his family, suddenly he began to feel used and demanded more time for himself. He worried about younger men competing with him at work. He was balding and wondered if he was still attractive to other women. A friend near his age died and suddenly he saw his own mortality.

In his depression he started talking to another professional in the same line of work—an attractive, divorced woman. They were both vulnerable, and one thing led to another. Eventually, the woman called

Marian and told her she and Marian's husband were in love.

Marian fell apart. She confronted her husband. They fought bitterly and split up. He moved out and the woman moved in with him.

Marian was beside herself. Out of the blue her storybook life and marriage were over. But at least she still had her children. Or did she?

Her children, especially the two older ones who were now teenagers, blamed her for what had happened. From near perfect behavior, they suddenly became insulting and nasty to her. They swore at her and told her they hated her.

Marian was aghast. When she lost her husband, she had counted on the support of her children. Now she began to see that their love was being withheld. Their accusations began to make her rethink. Was she somehow responsible? Was she really to blame?

Instead of thinking it out clearly, she laid herself open to Stu and Kathleen where she was most vulnerable. She came to them, as they had come to her on so many occasions, and asked them to explain. She really wanted to know. Why did they blame her? What had she done wrong?

An adult may have seen Marian's pain and said the right things to comfort her. An adult may have pointed out that the children were hurting too. They loved their dad intensely and he had gone away from mom. Now they were afraid that he would go away from them as well. An adult may have told Marian that she was not in the least to blame, that it was just hard for the kids to experience this pain, that Marian should help the kids to understand that even though their father may seem to be rejecting them now, at a later point in his life, he would very likely become loving toward them again.

But the children, being basically inexperienced and feeling intense pain for probably the first time in their lives, responded selfishly. They ignored Marian's pain and focused entirely on their own.

They told Marian that the divorce was her fault. They blamed her because she had stayed at home and not gone out and sought a profession. They said she was at fault because she had become so *boring*. It was her being boring that had caused dad to leave and break up the family.

The kids' words struck home. Marian had been looking at herself and reappraising. She now faced reentering the job force and didn't have many marketable skills. In fact, she didn't seem to have a remote possibility of making anywhere the kind of money her husband could make. She had been thinking that staying home and caring for the kids all those years had been a definite mistake.

And now the kids reaffirmed those thoughts. They continued to tell her that she was at fault. They got out of their chores by moping around. They pointed out that other children had two parents to manage the house and they were being asked to do more because they did not. When she accepted what they told her, they took it as a sign of weakness and only increased their pressure. As a result, Marian tried to take on both parents' roles and became exhausted, fatigued, and cranky. She and the kids were miserable.

Sorting Things Out

Marian finally sought professional help. When she came in to see Dr. deGarcia, Marian was very confused. She had done what both she and her husband had decided. She had lived a lifestyle that had seemed perfect and had resulted in a wonderful family. Yet, she had ended up losing her husband and now she had come to believe it was her fault. She also believed it was her fault that her children seemed to hate her and were having such a difficult time.

Marian's first question was, "What did I do wrong?" The answer, which Marian discovered in the course of her therapy, was that she had done nothing wrong. She had made all the right moves and still she had an unhappy result.

Life plays by its own rules. It threw her husband into a midlife crisis that shattered their marriage. Was it her fault? Was her becoming "boring" the cause of his problem?

Hardly. She had done what they both agreed she should do. She wasn't boring. She had been active, taking classes and redecorating. She was the wife he had always said he wanted her to be. He changed.

Marian came to see that she wasn't to blame for the children's hurt either. It was the fear of totally losing their dad that was driving the kids. But they didn't understand that. They only wanted their dad back the way he was. When he wasn't there for them, they felt pain. Because of their narcissism, they couldn't see that Marian felt pain as well, and they lashed out at her.

Not recognizing her own vulnerability in this situation—or her kids' ability to use that vulnerability against her—Marian made one mistake. When she was attacked by her children, she went to them for help. She didn't realize that when teens are hurting they want it to stop, immediately, regardless of the cost to anyone else. She didn't realize that although they were basically good kids, they wouldn't think of her best interests. They would think only of themselves.

Understanding all this, Marian might not have been so devastated by her children's actions and could have instead focused on the real problem, their fear of losing their father's love.

OVERT ANGER

Another common reaction by teens to divorce is just plain anger. A parent going through a divorce cannot always expect love and understanding from the teenager. The parent may be saying, "See it from my perspective. What could I do? I just couldn't stay in the situation any longer."

The teen, on the other hand, who sees the universe as moving around him or her, may be replying, "Why did you go and mess up my life? Things were going just swell for me. Now, suddenly you go and do this. I hate you for it!"

When teens find their lives disrupted by divorce, they can respond by making life intolerable for the parent with whom they live. By placing the blame for the pain they feel on the parent, they can feel perfectly justified in carrying out all sorts of terrible actions.

Stella

Marilyn left her husband when she found out he had been sleeping with their babysitter, ten years his junior. She felt there was no way she could stay married to the man, particularly since he didn't appear the least bit contrite or willing to change.

One day not long afterward she was feeling so low that she was crying to herself about the divorce. Stella, her daughter, walked in the room and Marilyn took a deep breath. "You have to be strong for Stella," she told herself.

She called her daughter over, intending to comfort her. She surmised that her daughter must feel as bad, if not worse, about the situation as she did.

Stella, however, refused her attention. Instead she screamed, "I hate you! You are the meanest mother in the world! Look what you have done to my dad. I'll get you for it!" She then turned and stormed out.

Marilyn had to catch herself to keep from fainting. Her lungs constricted and she felt she couldn't breathe. She later told Dr. deGarcia, "If I could have died on the spot, I would have been glad. If I had realized how my daughter was going to take it, I might not have left my husband at all. Look what I had done!"

After that, Stella expressed her anger in many ways. She began hanging around with wilder friends because she knew it upset her mom. When she wanted the freedom to stay out until 11 o'clock at night and Marilyn said no, Stella saw this as just another act of meanness on her mother's part.

When her dad remarried, Stella started getting close to her new stepmom. She hinted to her stepmom that she needed clothes because her real mom was very selfish and bought her very little. To emphasize this, whenever she visited her stepmom and dad, she would sneak out old tattered clothes. Then she'd take off the nice ones her mother had given, and don the old ones. Both her father and stepmom were taken in.

They thought the worst of Stella's real mother.

Finally, after a particularly pitiful episode in which Stella came over with a torn dress and shoes with holes in them, the stepmom suggested that Stella move in with dad. If she did, she would get wonderful new clothes and lots of attention.

That night when Marilyn came home from work, she innocently went to check in her daughter's room. All the clothes were gone, the room was bare.

Marilyn immediately called the stepmom's house, but no one answered. She kept trying and finally got hold of the dad. He refused to talk with her.

So Marilyn called the police and had Stella brought home.

Stella arrived, sullen and quiet. It was then that Marilyn realized she had lost control. Stella felt powerful. After all, look who was in her corner—her stepmom and her dad.

Stella called Marilyn all sorts of names. Then, sneering, walked out the door. When Marilyn went after her to bring her back, she saw her ex-husband sitting in his car with the motor running.

Marilyn gave up. She sent Stella to live with her father.

Dealing with the Anger

Marilyn concluded that it must all be her fault. She had wanted the divorce. She had insisted that Stella live with her. Stella's anger and acting up were mom's fault.

Marilyn continued to work, but she really didn't have a life. She didn't date; she didn't go out. She simply existed. Her guilt kept her pinned down like a ball and chain.

Meanwhile, things weren't really working out for Stella at school or at home. No matter what bad thing happened to her, she was convinced it was all because of her mom and the divorce. Eventually, she went to Dr. deGarcia for therapy.

Over time Dr. deGarcia worked with Stella to help to see her own narcissism. It was a long process . . . and painful. It's far easier to be angry at someone outside for causing the pain we feel than to think that the pain is normal.

Stella was made to see that the world was imperfect and it

wasn't set up for her benefit. Good things happen and sometimes bad things happen as well. It wasn't anyone's fault. It was just life and circumstance. Certainly it wasn't her mother's fault.

Finally, when she was twenty, Stella went to her mom and apologized. She admitted that Marilyn wasn't to blame. It was the pain of the divorce and her blindness to her mom's needs and feelings that made Stella act so angrily.

Marilyn didn't believe it, not at first. The guilt had been laid on so long that it had become a part of her. But eventually she came to see Stella's actions more clearly. She could see that Stella had been simply throwing a tantrum. Life had dealt Stella a curve and, rather than accept it, understand it, and go forward, Stella lashed out. It was the reaction of a wounded child.

If Marilyn had been able to see that earlier, she might have handled the first months after the divorce better. She might have been less emotional about losing her daughter to her ex-husband and his wife and realized that many times a child is just looking for the easy way out.

A big help would have been for Marilyn to have started making more of a life of her own and detaching from her daughter emotionally. That could have given her the objectivity she needed to counteract the scenes Stella staged and to handle her anger firmly and calmly.

DIVORCE AND MONEY

Divorce almost always creates an immediate money problem. Suddenly the same amount of money must support two households instead of one. This necessitates adjustments and cutting back in lots of areas.

Children, however—particularly teenagers—are very sensitive about any financial cutbacks. Money has become extremely important to them. They want albums and tapes, lipsticks, creams and other beauty products, fashionable clothes, a car to drive, cash for eating out ("You can't expect me to bring my lunch to high school!"), and much more. Money, a lot of it, is essential for many teenage lifestyles.

When divorce suddenly tightens the purse strings, the result can be teen anger. The narcissistic teen may simply not see the problems the parents are facing. All that matters is getting the allowance or the keys to the car.

Jane

Jane and her husband decided to handle their divorce in as grown-up a fashion as possible. They worked out a financial arrangement that gave them each enough to survive on. The father told their three children that he loved them and respected their mother, but that he needed to live away from her. He also explained that he had grown very fond of one of mom's friends and probably would be bringing her with him on his visitations to see them.

Even though it was a painful divorce, it was probably the best arrangement under the circumstances. Jane knew it could be far worse.

The Teen Perspective

But the three teenagers did not see it that way. Mom immediately cut out all allowances. She explained they were strapped for money and that she just couldn't afford to give them any. She suggested that they each go out and get jobs. They only saw that they wouldn't have the monetary things they used to have. That made them angry.

They were, of course, concerned about mom and dad and they hated the idea of divorce. But they were also concerned with maintaining the images they had created for themselves in front of their peers . . . and working and not having money just didn't fit in.

So, they got together and talked it out and actually worked out a plan to get what they wanted. They knew how much their mother loved them and they figured that because she was a working mother, she would be easy to manipulate. Seemingly independently, each began to ask for immediate things, such as new clothes, dancing lessons, a bedroom set.

Jane, seeing that the requests came from each of the children, assumed that this was some sort of need that each had, perhaps a way to compensate for the pain of the divorce. But there was no way that she could afford what the children wanted on her current salary.

But Jane was very bright and she decided to become more successful professionally. She would solve the problem by making more money ... and she did. She had an accounting background, so she began handling accounts for people she knew. She took courses and became more familiar with the business and took on more clients. She hired a housekeeper and used the time saved to devote to her business.

Jane had a magic touch and very soon she had increased her income. But it all went to the kids. They seemed to be bottomless pits when it came to financial demands.

So Jane increased her income again and again. She hired a gardener and a woman to come in and cook. She used the time saved to get more clients by entertaining and giving free speeches to local clubs and service groups in her area.

Each time the demands from the kids sucked away all her money. With her magic touch, she became quite well-known professionally and she made lots of money. But she had nothing to show for it since it all went to her kids.

Jane carried the children until they were all in their twenties. But she wasn't happy about it. She felt bullied, overworked, tired, and just plain sorry for herself. She also felt guilty because she thought that to be a good parent she should provide everything her children wanted. No matter how much she gave, however, it was never enough.

Learning to Say No

When she came to see Dr. deGarcia for therapy, Jane felt that she was trapped. She really didn't want to have to work so hard to make all that money and she wanted to have more fun in life, but what could she do? There were the children to think about.

It took Jane a while to realize that the children had manipulated her into confusing love with money. They had worked on her natural guilt over the divorce and blown it up in her mind.

She had lost her husband and deep inside, no matter what the real circumstances, she couldn't help but blame herself. The kids had simply encouraged her to go on believing this.

Deep down she also felt guilt at the pain the kids suffered because of the divorce. The children had really worked on this, ultimately convincing Jane that the only relief for their pain was monetary.

When Jane finally realized that the kids only saw her as a provider, she began to shuck off some of her guilt. She realized that by giving them money and things money could buy, she wasn't winning their love. She was just feeding their narcissism. She also realized that she did not have to feel guilty about the divorce. It was not her fault.

She had allowed her children to make her feel guilty because she had defined the parent role so narrowly. She needed to realize that being a good parent means more than providing for children, it means giving them good quality time. With this new realization, she became guilt-free and shared *herself* with her children instead of all her money.

Jane ultimately asked all her children to move out and went to Europe, by herself, for two months. This was the best thing she could have done not only for herself, *but for her children.*

It is often very difficult to choose yourself over your children, especially if you're a divorced parent. More often than not, divorced parents make their children "over-valued," giving them too much time and money and too much of themselves.

The solution is to work at putting the situation into perspective by saying "no" more often, by being more selfish, by helping your children to see that you need support, help, and time to yourself. If you do this, then you'll begin to establish better priorities for your children and they will become less selfish.

On the other hand, if you allow them to suck you dry, they may become people who will never be satisfied or who never recognize another person's needs.

Try it! Live your life and let your children be part of it, not all of it.

THE HARM TEEN FANTASIES CAN DO

Thus far we've discussed teens who have blamed one parent or the other for the immediate pain caused by divorce. But in a sense, we've only scratched the surface of the problem. It can go far deeper, such as when the child doesn't fully realize what he or she is doing. This can be the case with teen fantasies.

We all fantasize at one time or another and to a greater or lesser degree. But teen fantasies can be very elaborate. After all, the world is open to teenagers. They can easily imagine being queen of the ball, a Marine captain, president of a company, or even President of the U.S. Their dreams have not been tainted by reality. School, teachers, and parents have encouraged them to be all they can be. Many times they do not know their limits because the real world of competition, money, and politics is totally foreign to them. (In part this is good because it allows them to imagine a future toward which they can build.)

But unrealistic fantasies can be harmful to teenagers, because they tie in with the child's natural narcissism. They can take strange twists, and cause the child to confuse dreams with reality.

Myra

Sandra married an older man, a divorcee who had children. She liked the fact that he seemed so stable and he really loved his children.

Her own rapport with his four children, the oldest of whom was a teenager, was great. She was young enough that they almost considered her one of their crowd. The kids seemed to think of her more as a friend than a stepmom and Sandra liked this.

Everything seemed to be going well until Sandra became pregnant.

Once her own baby was born, the teenager, Myra, began to show signs of jealousy. Myra, as the oldest child, had always been the focal point of the children in the family.

But now, Sandra and the baby seemed to be getting too much attention. Myra, feeling jealous, began to try to win the attention of her father away from Sandra. She began commenting on her stepmom's "sagging bottom," her aging, and her stomach that wasn't as flat as it had been before having the baby. She gleefully cuddled up to her father in front of Sandra whenever possible.

Sandra complained about the behavior to the girl's natural mother, who was supportive of Sandra. Both women spoke to the father and they all agreed that it was a problem caused both by the divorce and by the birth of Sandra's new baby. They agreed that the solution was to give Myra more attention for the time being. Once she felt secure, they believed that the problems would vanish by themselves.

Myra, however, did not see the circumstances as did the adults. She only saw that suddenly she was getting attention again. Eyes were focusing on her instead of the baby, particularly her father's. So her behavior continued.

Eventually the entire family went in to a counselor. He told the father to be sure not to reject Myra, because for whatever reason she felt replaced by the new baby. Myra just wasn't getting as much attention from Sandra as she had before, so dad had to make up the difference.

Making Things Worse

When dad responded even more to Myra's attentions, the girl totally misunderstood the circumstances. She began to fantasize that her father was unhappy with her stepmom. Myra began to dream that since the child arrived, her father had lost his love for his new wife and was lonely, alone, and hurting (much the way Myra herself felt). Myra's narcissistic reasoning was that because she was unhappy, her dad must be unhappy too.

As a result, Myra decided that what she must do is give her father all her love. She began to see herself in direct competition with her stepmom for her father's love. She focused all her attention on him, and was physically playful and affectionate. She hung on him whenever she could, even flirted with him.

The father, acting on the counselor's advice and with the consent of both his current and ex-wife, responded by being attentive to Myra "for her own good."

Inevitably one of Myra's friends' parents noticed this behavior and was horrified. This person called social welfare and said they suspected sexual abuse. The father and stepmother were hauled in. The father protested his innocence, but he was told that was what any guilty man in his circumstances would do. Sandra felt guilty. Here she had been encouraging her husband to pay more attention to his 16-year-old daughter, never realizing that the girl's fantasies about her father's unhappiness would lead to such problems.

Sandra's husband, *who actually did nothing wrong,* felt much the same way. First he thought of himself as a fool. Then he felt guilty for not realizing what was going on. He felt that it was his fault. His feelings of guilt were reinforced by our culture, which is set up to always blame the man in these circumstances.

A Resolution with Time

Eventually Sandra and her husband convinced the authorities of his innocence. Myra finally confessed that she had flirted with her dad to make Sandra jealous. She explained that she did it simply because she wanted her dad to herself. Once she was again the center of attention, she just couldn't back down. She was so wrapped up in her fantasy, she lost touch with the real consequences of her actions.

A MORAL FOR STEPPARENTS

Stepparents often feel guilty when children have difficulty coping with their new families and overcompensate. They feel they've brought the children pain, so they must do everything they can to help alleviate that pain.

In the process they forget that the children have minds of their own. They can be clever, vengeful, and, in this circumstance, can even come to believe their own fantasies.

In normal times parents would never let the teenager get away with the sort of thing that occurs in and around a divorce. But because of the special circumstances they go out of their way to overlook problems and underestimate the child's part in what happens.

What parents and stepparents need to realize is that the more they feel guilty, the more likely they are to take some self-defeating action. In this case guilt caused Sandra and her husband to unwittingly play along with Myra's mistaken ideas about her father.

And here's another hint for stepparents: it's usually better to move in slowly and not try to change everything too fast. It's important to always consider that the stepchildren were raised by another person. As a general rule it is better not to discipline, lecture, nag, or try to change them too fast, if at all. It is better to become an advisor, as Sandra tried to do. Remember, it takes a long time to build trust and while it is building, most children will test you. Move slowly.

USING THE TRIANGLE

Another fairly common ploy that teenagers of divorce use to get their own way is to set up a triangle, pitting their parents against each other, against stepparents, or against grandparents. Teens understand that divorce naturally creates divisiveness among the adults involved, and they instinctively use that to their own advantage.

Triangles can be set up many different ways, but it's always a parent who's caught in the middle: A son tells his father that his stepfather has promised him a home computer and the father must decide whether to vie with the stepfather for the boy's affections by buying expensive toys. A daughter tells her mother that her stepfather punished her needlessly, and the mother must side with one or the other.

The key to handling these triangles is good communication between the adults involved. They must realize that the teenager is using them as weapons against each other and must work together to disarm the teen.

Communication and cooperation can be tough, of course, if the teenager has chosen to pit his natural parents against each other, particularly if the divorce was a bitter one. But it can also be difficult when the child sets up the triangle within a good marriage or between parents and grandparents.

Grant

Sandy was thirty-two years old. She had one stepson, Grant, who was thirteen. For five years she had been raising him, and everything seemed to be going along all right. (Grant's natural mom had moved to another state with her new husband and wanted to be left alone to start a new life. So this left Sandy, the stepmother, to care for Grant.)

However, thirteen was the magic age. Grant went to the movies and saw a show about a dad and his son making it by themselves in society. (The mother in the movie had died and the boy became the center of his dad's world.) The relationship between the two was so wonderful that Grant romanticized the movie into his own life.

As an American teenager, he was coming up against the real world in school, with his peers, with life in general. Suddenly he was no longer able to control things the way he wanted.

On the other hand, in the movie with just the father and son living together, things had worked out perfectly. The father had been so attentive to the son's needs and wants that the movie boy got everything.

Grant so identified with the movie that he decided he wanted his life to be that way. He wanted to be alone with his dad. The only thing in the way was his stepmom.

Grant began coming to the table with his hands and face dirty. He talked with his mouth full. He left his clothes around, and, not so secretly, he broke the top off Sandy's jewelry box.

For Sandy and Grant's father, the behavior was a mystery. The boy had always been loved and cared for in a healthy manner and no one understood his new actions.

It fell upon Sandy, however, being home most with Grant, to do the disciplining. She found she had to increase her discipline enormously in order to try to maintain control. This made her look like a "bitch," in Grant's words.

Sandy tried to reprimand him in a fair and consistent way. But some of the things he did were so sneaky that when he denied it, it began to look to Grant's father as if Sandy were picking on the boy.

Grant stepped up the pressure by appealing to his natural grandparents. He began to make up stories about how Sandy was trying to hurt him physically. If he bruised himself accidentally, he would blame her for it.

Grant did not realize what he was doing, did not know the impact he would cause. He was attached to his dad and just wanted to see more of him.

Things grew increasingly worse. Sandy was having to constantly defend herself to her husband's parents. Her husband, unaware of what was really going on, found himself unable to always side with Sandy. Each time he sided with Grant or with his own parents, it drove another wedge into their marriage.

Eventually, after one brutal argument in which Grant's grandparents drove up to the home to help defend Grant, Sandy gave up. She left.

Now Grant had what he wanted. His father, deeply feeling the loss of Sandy, had no one to turn to but Grant. And Grant responded warmly to his father's attention.

For the poor father it was a kind of trap. Grant was right there ready to fill the gap. It was an easy, comfortable thing to do. Just let Grant make up the loneliness in his life. The dad took Grant everywhere, made meals for him at home, helped him with schoolwork, allowed him to leave his room (and the house) a mess, and gave him a big allowance.

It was terrific for Grant at first. He had what he later described as one of the best times ever.

But after a while, Grant began to resent the demands for emotional support his father placed on him. Getting disgusted with his dad, he told him what he had done. He explained how he had cleverly engineered the separation, splitting Sandy off from the family.

Dad was, of course, shocked and dismayed. He got in touch with Sandy and started working to save the marriage. Grant was sent to his grandparents for a while until the two parents could bond and communicate better.

How the Problem Could Have Been Avoided

The real problem here was a lack of understanding on the part of Sandy and her husband. They were both loving parents, deeply in love with each other. They wanted only the best for the family. What they failed to fully comprehend was how clever, how sneaky, and how devious Grant could be.

They were done in by their memories of him as a sweet, innocent child. They did not realize that when he became a teenager, he would have an adult mind and adult capabilities being driven by a narcissistic personality.

If only they had realized that Grant was doing his very best to control his environment for selfish reasons, the outcome might have been different. United with the knowledge of what Grant was really doing, Sandy and dad could have avoided the triangle created between Sandy and the grandparents. The parents could have explained the boy's behavior to the grandparents instead of falling victim to it. *Understanding* what was going on would have undoubtedly thwarted Grant's actions.

This is not to say that Grant was evil or even to blame. Grant was only doing what was natural. He saw the world through his own eyes. Things had been going his way for so long that he couldn't conceive of a world where things did not go his way.

It would have been beneficial for Grant if Sandy and her husband had seen through his manipulation. It would have been educational for him to learn that he could not control his home environment.

Yes, it would have been painful. And he would undoubtedly have thrown the sort of tantrums that teenagers are noted for. But the normal pain would have matured him and he would have become a far healthier adult.

FROM THE INSIDE

It's important to understand how difficult it is to analyze the situation from within. It's one thing to look at the stories we've retold from the outside and say, "Uh-huh, he (or she) should have seen it coming."

But when you're in the situation, it's so much harder. That's why parents in a divorce must be ever vigilant for the manipulations of children.

For parents in a divorced family, the greatest enemy is naivete. Sometimes you just don't realize what you're up against.

Your greatest strength, on the other hand, is knowledge. Knowing what the kids are capable of, knowing that they can do terrible things (for reasons that are innocent—to them) can put you in a position of power. It can free you of guilt so that you can then help your children cope with their pain and come to accept the changes brought on by divorce.

8
Outside Influences

It never dawns on many parents that their lives and those of their children can be drastically affected by someone outside their home and family. They don't realize that doctors, judges, school counselors, therapists, even neighbors and other parents, can sometimes override their authority or counteract their impact on their own children—even when the family is not in crisis or hasn't sought outside help.

But outsiders—whether they're well-intentioned but misdirected "buttinskies," public authorities acting on limited information, or good people who have learned to think the worst through news stories of child abuse and other horrors—can have a serious impact on your child's development.

And they're often aided in this by children's ability to tell tales. Even children raised in loving, warm homes may twist the truth to win outsiders' sympathy or fabricate stories about their parents to cover up some misdeed of their own.

In this chapter we'll consider the problems of families that suffer because of the intervention of someone outside the family. In some cases, an outsider listens to the stories of children and then contributes to the creation of a family crisis. In others, people in positions of authority misinterpret a situation or give bad advice.

Either way, the problem is not caused directly by the parents. Rather, it is the circumstances and the introduction of an outside element that is upsetting.

If you recognize yourself here in various roles, don't be alarmed. The purpose is to inform and educate. Once you see what can happen, you will be far less likely in the future to find yourself under the control of outsiders.

CHILDREN WHO LIE

The fact is that children do sometimes lie about their parents, and there are people out there ready to support the lies the children may tell. It's important that you understand both parts of this dynamic, so let's begin by finding out why children tell stories about their parents.

The rationale behind many children's lies is to get the parent in trouble with someone else. That other person could be another relative, other parents, or even the authorities. In the children's narcissistic eyes, lying is simply another technique to use to get what they want. Until they've felt some of the pain it can produce, they simply aren't aware they are doing anything wrong.

For example, one three-and-a-half-year-old went from

house to house in his neighborhood telling the neighbors how he hated his mother because she never fixed him any breakfast or lunch. When the concerned neighbors asked him why that was so, he explained that it was punishment because he hadn't eaten all of his sandwich last week. He went on to explain that he was hungry and if they had any dessert handy, he would be happy to eat it.

The child obviously had made it all up to get even with a mother who insisted that he finish his lunch.

WHY ADULTS BELIEVE LIES

A few years ago, it was easy to laugh at such stories, even at more sophisticated lies from older children. But over the last few years we have increasingly been exposed to the very real problem of child abuse. The news media, films, documentaries, and books have deluged us with stories of beatings and sexual abuse of children until today most of us are ready to believe the worst.

The truth, however, is that while child abuse does occur and must be guarded against, we have become oversensitized to it. Thus whenever any child makes any kind of statement about abuse, the presumption of guilt immediately falls upon the parents and they must defend themselves.

This is not, of course, to say that we as adults should ignore any plea for help from children of any age or that we should be less vigilant in guarding against true abuse. It is to say, however, that we must balance what we hear against our common sense. We must not immediately assume the parent is wrong and the child is being abused. It could be exactly the other way around.

THE WELL-MEANING GRANDPARENT

Although you might think otherwise, one of the most common targets of a child's lies is a grandparent.

One mother, Gwen, experienced this problem firsthand when her son Donny was only three years old. The boy had constant temper tantrums. When put to bed, he would tear apart everything in his room. He would eat only what he wanted and refuse anything else.

The mother insisted on cleanliness in his room and wanted the boy to eat a balanced diet. So the boy looked around to see if there were some means to get his way.

Gwen's mother-in-law babysat while both parents worked. When she arrived, she would ask the boy why he was acting so strangely. He explained with stories. He told her his mother didn't really want to play with him or work with him, so she locked him in his bedroom. He said he was acting up and refusing to eat because his mother was so mean to him.

The grandmother sided with the child. She fed him "big" breakfasts of his favorite foods (mostly sugar items). When she did, she was rewarded with hugs and kisses and comments such as, "I want you to stay forever!"

This only caused the mother to try to be stricter with the child, which resulted in the grandparent cajoling and spoiling him even more.

Eventually terrible arguments ensued between mother and grandmother. These were made worse by the fact that Donny, like other small children, had a fine line between fantasy and reality. Soon the child began to really believe that his mother had done all sorts of terrible things to him. He became confused about what was real and what wasn't.

In the meantime the grandmother put terrible pressure on the mother. Of course, mom knew she was innocent, but the accusations hurt and she began to be more lenient with the boy. She fed him things he liked, rather than things that were good for him. Ultimately, he got his way.

In this case, the outside element was the grandmother. The child parlayed her misguided interference into *getting his own way.*

IT GETS HARDER, NOT EASIER

In the above example we used the case of a three-year-old to show that even young children can manipulate parents using the weapon of an outsider. As the child gets older, however, the weapon can be wielded in a more sophisticated fashion.

Richard

Linda and her husband had an eleven-year-old who was simply fed up with household obligations. Linda insisted that Richard take out the trash, make his bed, and otherwise clean up, but these duties did not fit in at all with his concept of the universe. He saw himself as a sort of prince and his parents as his servants.

At first Richard did the chores while complaining about them. But eventually he found a friend's mom who listened to his complaining. This encouraged him and he began to embellish his stories.

He told his friend's mom how hard his parents were on him and that they were alcoholics. (They had an occasional drink at parties.) He claimed they really didn't care what happened to him. He said they made him pay for everything and that his allowance didn't even cover his lunches at school.

This substitute mom was divorced and living alone with her son. She herself was lonely and empathized with Richard. He received sympa-thy, caring, and understanding from her. She was a good person and wanted to help, so she spent more and more time with him, making cookies, playing, and generally having a good time. He liked her and she liked him.

For Richard, it was heaven-sent—a new mom who really understood him. The woman just saw it as doing a good deed for a poor boy whose parents didn't understand him as well as she did. She thought perhaps she was doing them a favor by being there for him.

Eventually Richard had a fight with his parents and went to his friend's house to spend the night. He didn't call home. His parents, nat-urally, were worried. At about midnight they finally guessed where he might have gone. Just before calling the police, the mother called the substitute mom's house.

Because of the boy's lies about his parents, the woman tried to pro-tect Richard by denying he was there. But something about what she said made Linda suspicious, so her husband got on the phone. Getting angry, he told the woman that he knew she was not telling the truth. He said they were coming right over to get the boy and that he'd better be ready to go. He also gave her a piece of his mind.

This made the woman wonder if Richard had been right all along. She now felt that she needed to help him communicate better with his family, especially his father.

When Linda and her husband got there, the other mom tried to block them. She stood in the doorway and refused to let them enter, hoping to calm them down first.

Linda's husband, however, was not to be daunted. He called for Rich-ard to come out and sooner rather than later.

The boy, who had been hiding behind the doorway, realized that things were getting out of hand. It was becoming a lot scarier than he had bargained for. So, sheepishly, he came out the door and went to his parents.

They took him home and grounded him for two weeks. During that time he finally confessed his manipulative behavior and they found out the whole story. They were shocked to learn that for over a year he had been laying the groundwork by telling the friend's mom made-up sto-ries.

Richard's parents decided to talk with the woman themselves. After an hour or two of conversation, all three realized that they should have communicated sooner because they all had Richard's best interests at heart.

THE MORAL

Parents, there are sometimes people out there who may believe your children's lies about you. Perhaps these people have had unhappy circumstances in their own lives and are unwilling to trust parents in general. Whatever the reason, some of these people are willing to interfere to protect your poor child against your "bullying."

Most parents are innocents in this area. They think they have the support of other parents and society in general, as long as they're loving and caring parents. This simply isn't the case. The truth is that many people are willing to believe the worst about parents.

INFLUENCES AT SCHOOL

That we are often the brunt of others' worst suspicions is born out by the case of Dan and his two sons. Here is an instance where the child told no lies and did nothing wrong. Yet outsiders nevertheless forced their way into the situation. It is a classic case of trying to fix something that wasn't broken.

Dan came to Dr. deGarcia for counseling because he wanted to feel better about himself. The question that he was encouraged to begin with was, "Did the change make a difference?"

Dan

Dan's two sons were nine and ten when he and his wife divorced. The younger boy went to live with his mother while the older lived with Dan. It seemed a reasonable resolution.

Dan devoted his life to his sons. He worked with his older boy all the time and with the younger boy on weekends. He taught them both to play golf. He took them skiing and listened to their problems.

After four years the older boy began to have trouble in school. He excelled in athletics (largely because Dan had coached and taught him) but academics gave him trouble. He was well liked both by his peers and by adults, but he simply could not seem to concentrate well enough to get good grades.

The boy had not excelled in grammar school either, but the problem was not so dramatic there. As he got into the sixth, seventh, and eighth grades and the work got harder, however, he fell further and further behind. By the time the boy was in the ninth grade, he was failing badly. It was then that the teachers decided to do something about it.

Dan had tried to raise this son (and the younger son on weekends) in as healthy a manner as possible. He saw that both his boys were good-looking and popular. As they grew older they seemed to become happier and happier. The only problem was that the older boy did poorer and poorer in school.

The comparison was made between the two boys. The younger son had good grades. They had virtually the same teachers. The older was failing. Where was the problem?

The teachers felt that the difference was in parenting. They felt that Dan was simply too lax with the older boy. The father wasn't forcing the boy to work hard enough.

The teachers confronted Dan. They told him that the problem was that he simply wasn't a good enough parent. Dan was simply too unconcerned about life and the boy had picked this up. The boy was following in Dan's footsteps. That was the reason he was goofing off at school and getting bad grades.

Dan listened to everything that was said and took it to heart. He, after all, only wanted what was best for his son. At the suggestion of one of the teachers and with the blessing of his ex-wife, he agreed to give up custody. His son would go to live with the mother and, hopefully, learn enough responsibility to do well in school.

Dan rarely saw his sons after that. Told by both the school and his ex-wife that he had caused his son's problems, he didn't want to hurt his sons anymore. But Dan felt great pain and loss over having to give up the boy.

As it turned out, the older son did not do better with the mother. However, mom and the teachers continued to point the finger of blame at Dan because the boy seemed to lack so many primary skills.

Finally, after seven months of therapy, Dan began to realize that perhaps it wasn't actually his fault. The boy had always had a poor attention span. Maybe it was just a situation where this child would not do well in school, ever.

Dan went to the school to investigate. In the year since Dan had given up his son, the young man had done even more poorly than before. Worse, the boy was perpetually unhappy without his father.

Dan began to realize that he had not caused his son's difficulty in school. He had done the best for his son and the boy's previous happy personality had confirmed that. It was simply the case that the boy was a "C-" student.

Dan released his guilt and regained his self-respect. He asked for his son back. The boy was now old enough to tell the judge his choice and went happily back to his dad. His grades never did become great, but he was a happy, healthy young man.

INVITE OUTSIDERS IN

In this example, the teachers at school interfered and defined a problem where one did not exist. Then they started looking for the cause. In a divorce situation, the cause seemed to jump out at them—a poor parent.

Both well-meaning outsiders like these teachers and people who are simply meddlesome buttinskies think they have the true interests of the child at heart. The trouble is that frequently the problem is a figment of the child's imagination or, as in this situation, no problem at all.

Still, those outside the family frequently walk all over parents, creating far more damage than they realize.

The way to avoid some of the problems of buttinskies is to know your children's friends and the parents of these friends. Invite some of these people to your house, particularly any who seem to have a strong influence on your child. Do a little detective work about the people who become a big part of your child's life. Get to know them and let them get to know you.

QUESTION AUTHORITY

When it comes to outside influences, those in apparent authority can have the most impact. The reason is simple. When things go wrong, parents first blame themselves. They beat their chests, mumble "mea culpa," and worry that they didn't toilet train properly or that they forced their children to eat solid cereal too early.

All that's needed is for someone "in authority" to confirm their worst suspicions and it's off the deep end. Let a psychologist say, "You're to blame" and it's all over. After all, if the authority says it, it has to be right.

In the last example we saw how teachers could act as authority figures to cause a good man to give up a good son. However, there are those who have far higher places of authority and for whom you must watch out even more closely.

Kathy

After much denying it, Gretta finally admitted that her brown-eyed, raven-haired, lovely girl, Kathy, was doing very poorly in intermediate school and with her entire life.

Kathy glared at her parents and talked back. She hung around with the "wrong crowd," seemed to sleep all the time, was irritable when awake, and then blamed all her problems on her mother. Gretta began to suspect that her daughter was experimenting with drugs.

Kathy had always been a bright, loving, and good all-around child. She had been happy and had loved sports, dancing, and modeling. But in her last portfolio for modeling, Gretta saw something that she had never seen before—deep sunken eyes, a sullen smile, and defiant looks.

Kathy had always been in classes for the gifted and had done well . . . until now. Now she complained that the teachers were picking on her. "They hate me," she would say.

Her dress was terrible. She would wear the same four outfits to school each week.

At the time, Gretta and her husband were going through a divorce. Her mother-in-law blamed the girl's problem on Gretta, because she was divorcing her son.

But Gretta felt that the divorce alone could not be it. Both her ex-husband and she agreed that the divorce was necessary and better. Gretta was dating a man who adored the kids and everything seemed to be going well there. The other children were doing well. It was only Kathy who seemed to be having problems.

Both Gretta and her ex-husband were confused. They felt they had loved the child properly. But because of Kathy's actions, they began to blame themselves and feel guilty. Even though they knew it was not the right thing, they even began to consider reconciliation for the sake of the girl.

Instead, Gretta decided to take positive action directly. She moved Kathy to a different public school, one which had a great many more activities and where, she felt, Kathy's modeling would be enhanced. She started the girl in soccer and softball. Kathy, however, did not change. She did not stick to any sport (even though she had previously played sports for years).

Finally Gretta met with the school counselor. She had expected full cooperation from the school and the counselor, the people who were in "authority" and presumably knew what to do to help.

Instead of support, however, she received condemnation. She was told "common wisdom" truths about her bad "parenting style." She was asked, "What do you expect? You're getting a divorce. That screws up all children."

The counselor, in effect, told Gretta that she was to blame. What was worse, the counselor now took all the psychological information she had gained and used it against Kathy. She explained her views of the situation to all Kathy's teachers.

After that Kathy began being treated like she was neurotic. The teachers took notes of anything she did wrong. In effect, the counselor had diagnosed the situation and had come in with a verdict. Now Kathy was "branded" and Gretta was filled with guilt.

From Kathy's perspective, things seemed to be getting worse. She felt like a loser and she noticed the teachers were looking at her kind of "weird."

BAD ADVICE

There are some psychologists and counselors out there who take two-dimensional looks at very complex situations. This is sometimes the case within schools when someone makes a psychological generalization about a family, a parent, or a child's problem. How sad it is, for instance, to realize that many educators and counselors feel sorry for *all* children of divorce. Maybe it isn't always that bad.

The unfortunate thing is many times the counselor's opinion is not questioned. What these authorities say can cloud or misdirect a situation. They can make a parent feel guilty, especially if the parent is at wit's end with the child.

Sometimes schools have a sort of underground network along which information about students and their parents is passed. This network can blackball parents and make them ineffectual when dealing with school authorities. And since children then get the same message from all their teachers, it can convince them there's something wrong with them, that they're "no good."

The result is usually that both parents and child begin to feel worse about themselves. The advice given is sometimes irrelevant or even harmful. Ultimately, the situation deteriorates, which causes only more blaming.

TAKING CHARGE

In the above situation with Gretta and Kathy, however, things didn't get totally out of hand. Fortunately, Gretta was able to take Kathy out of public school and start again in a totally fresh environment. This time no one, particularly the school psychologist, knew that the family had a "defined problem."

Surprising to Gretta, Kathy suddenly changed. The child reversed herself. She came out as the star of the school and was loved and admired.

Nevertheless, the question remained, Why had Kathy acted the way she did? The answer didn't come out until the child was seventeen.

Then in counseling with Dr. deGarcia she revealed that a distant relative had tried to sexually molest her. She was scared and retreated after the incident. Because it was a relative, she was afraid to tell anyone.

It had all become very confusing for her. She just wanted to get away. She wanted to live with her friends.

Trying to turn away from her family, she found herself taken to a school psychologist. Then her teachers started treating her differently and began looking at her in a pitiful manner. She knew they were feeling sorry for her, but didn't know why.

She also began to hear innuendos from her school counselor about her mother not being supportive. The counselor suggested that maybe she might like to say how angry she was at her mother.

But Kathy felt good about her parents even though they were divorcing. Nevertheless, the counselor seemed to want her to blame them for her insecurities.

Finally, when she got to a new school, things seemed better. At the new school they didn't know about her background and they treated her normally. With the attention off, she was able to relax and focus on the real problem, which she was eventually able to express.

If Kathy had been encouraged to talk to her parents, things might have worked out sooner and easier. Talking makes the child feel less alone, less unique, and presents her with new options.

Kathy's parents, also, could have visited the classroom when they began to feel something was wrong. Many times if you make yourself more visible, particularly if you become involved with parent groups affiliated with the schools, you can influence educators on ways to handle your child.

Most people are surprised to learn how naive counselors, teachers, and even some therapists can be when it comes to children and guilt. Often these "experts" do not look deep enough to see the real problem. Frequently they just plug the child-parent into an already developed scenario. Too often they simply do not realize that the child has logical reasons for acting the way she or he does—molestation in this case.

Beware of authorities who make a ten-minute analysis and

then give a generalization. If you believe the generalization, it could live with you and your child for the rest of your lives.

AUTHORITIES IN HIGH PLACES

The problems with misdirected interference go all the way up the ladder of authority to the doctors, the social workers, and the judges. These are the real authority figures because they have the power to directly affect our lives. But just because they are in that position of power does not mean that they always have access to all the needed information or have the wisdom of Solomon. They are human, too. Sometimes they may be as much victims of "common wisdom" psychological generalization as anyone else.

Henry

After his divorce, Henry tried to get custody of his children. He lost. Nevertheless, the children were so important to him that he tried desperately to be a part of their lives. When he had them on weekends, he would take them places, lavish them with attention and gifts, and make them feel very special.

This, however, made life difficult for his ex-wife. After one particularly hard week of settling the kids down after a visit to Henry, she drove over to his house and had it out with him. She said the girls only complained that they wanted to stay longer with him. He was spoiling them and they wouldn't do anything that she said. He was upsetting them and giving them a terrible outlook on life. She wanted him to stop seeing them. Henry said no.

But the wife talked Henry into seeing a therapist. The therapist concurred with the wife and suggested that Henry should stay away from the girls. When Henry was still reluctant, the wife took the matter to court, where the judge limited Henry in his custody rights to one day a week.

Brokenhearted, Henry agreed with his wife not to see the children at all. He wanted the best for his children. His ex-wife, the therapist, and now even the judge concurred that his association with the children was harmful. Therefore, it must be so.

Henry went his way, trying to remake his life, living alone, working, and feeling sad.

When Trouble Finally Comes

Then one night months later he was awakened by a call at three in the morning from a local hospital. He was half asleep and couldn't understand the accusatory language from the nurse. He finally realized that one of his daughters was in trouble and rushed to the hospital.

When he got there he found out that the girl had just given birth to a premature baby boy. Henry, who hadn't seen the girl in seven months, was flabbergasted.

Henry wanted to immediately call his ex-wife, but the girl protested, saying, "No, Daddy. I don't want Mommy to ever know." She said she wanted to get away from her mother and when she couldn't go to Henry, she got pregnant so that she and her boyfriend would have to get married. She said of her mother, "She'll kill me. I know it!"

Henry, confronted by his daughter's fear of her mother, was now completely confused. He felt the girl's mother should be told, but his daughter absolutely refused. Henry didn't know what to do and appealed to those who are supposed to know.

However, the doctor, the nurses, and the social worker assigned to the case were unsympathetic. They continually badgered Henry with questions about why he didn't know that his daughter was pregnant. Why had he had no contact with her for those many months? Why had he "walked away from his responsibilities?" What did that say about his ability to be a good father?

They also wanted to know why the mother didn't know. The best answer they came up with was that the girl wore clothing to cover up the baby and that she didn't get very big because of her body structure. The truth may be that the mother simply didn't want to see. If you do not want to see something negative, you can go a long time without seeing it.

Henry tried to explain, saying that the therapist and his ex-wife had said he should stay away from the children. But now everyone said that was only a cop out. He should have known what was best and done the right thing regardless of what anyone had said. A "good" parent wouldn't have walked out of his children's lives. A "good" parent would have maintained contact with the children, regardless.

Trying to Resolve a Muddle

All the while he had been getting frantic phone calls from his ex-wife. Where was the daughter? Did he know? He wanted to explain to his ex-wife what had happened, but the daughter again pleaded with him not to tell her, so he was caught in the middle. Finally, he convinced the girl to call her mother.

When his ex-wife arrived, she blamed Henry for everything that had happened. She told him that he had to get out of the situation, that she would handle it from here. The doctor and the social worker concurred.

This time, however, Henry stood his ground. He felt he had abandoned his children once. Now, he felt his daughter was counting on him and he would not abandon her again. He told the mother that no matter what, the daughter was not going home with her.

The mother found there was little she could do. Her daughter now had a baby. The boyfriend wanted to marry the daughter (he was eight years older than her), and as soon as he did, the mother's legal power over the girl would evaporate. She could protest but do little else.

Henry saw the two children married and did everything he could to help them. He also went into therapy with Dr. deGarcia to try to alleviate the guilt and depression he felt.

He came to realize that it was the first therapist, the judge, and later the doctor, nurse, and social worker who had contributed to making the situation what it was. He had done nothing wrong. He had only loved his children and tried to be a good father.

Feeling better about himself, he insisted on and received the right from his ex-wife to see his other children more frequently and for longer periods of time. He began to see that he was not a terrible parent, but simply one who had been placed in a difficult situation. He cared. He loved. He wanted to do his best. And given half a chance, he could do it.

An epilogue to this story is that after many years and against the odds, the marriage between Henry's daughter and her boyfriend was succeeding and their child was doing well.

GETTING ADVICE YOU CAN TRUST

If there's a lesson to be learned here it is that the supposed authority of outsiders does not necessarily make them right. Whether it be therapist, judge, doctor, nurse, or social worker, quick judgments made on the basis of scant observations often lead to terrible advice. They may mean well, but the consequences may be disastrous for your family.

Of course, the question then arises, Whose advice can you take? If you can't rely on the person who is in a position of authority, who can you rely upon?

Here's the answer: Whenever an authority figure tells you that you are to blame, that you have done things wrong and are the cause of the bad consequences, and you can't see that you've done anything wrong, question that authority's conclusions.

Does that authority have a stake in the matter? Ex-husbands, ex-wives, and their relatives are often prejudiced, no matter how unbiased they may seem. Counselors and social workers, doctors and nurses, and even judges may have a vested interest in simply getting the situation resolved quickly so they can go onto the next item on their crowded agenda or they may have emotional issues around your circumstances because it reminds them of something in their own lives. With this kind of background, they may be inclined to go along with easy pop psychology generalizations that ultimately find you at fault.

Get another opinion, one that is impartial. It won't hurt and you can try it on to see if it feels right.

Test whatever is told to you. See how it feels, how it "wears." Just because someone wears the mantle of authority does not mean that they automatically have the right answer for you.

Decide if you're basically a loving, giving, caring parent. (If you've taken the time to read this book, then chances are you do care and do love.) If you love your children, then you know the guilt you feel whenever anything bad happens.

Does the outsider's advice add to your guilt or diminish it? If it adds to the guilt, regard what's said as suspect.

Remember, as a loving and caring parent you only want the best for your children. Undoubtedly you've done some things wrong, but they were probably done out of ignorance or out of a desire to protect your children and to give them a better life than you may have had.

That may make you an uninformed parent, but it does not mean that you are necessarily to blame when something bad happens. Stop kicking yourself. No one ever told you what parenting was going to be like. You were just thrown into the middle of it and told to sink or swim.

Remember, there's a payoff. You are part of a process that is forming another person to live in society. Yes, children are sometimes difficult, but they can also be an asset. They help you to build psychological character, help round off your sharp edges, and help you to be humble. They can give you moments of great joy. Each of us as parents has experienced the happiness of watching our child, our hearts and eyes filled with love and gratitude for what they have just done or said.

9
Sexual Abuse

Thus far in this book we have talked about situations where there is unnecessary guilt because parents have cared too much and have done everything within their power for their child. Because they've taken on full responsibility for their children, these parents have been overwhelmed by guilt. It is guilt without wrong being done.

But what if there *is* wrong? What if something terrible, such as child molestation, occurs? Can there still be unnecessary guilt? Can parents still suffer because of circumstances beyond their control?

In this chapter we'll examine unnecessary guilt when there has been child abuse.

A PROBLEM IN THE FAMILY

At the onset it's important to distinguish between child molestation that occurs outside a family and that which occurs within. When a child is molested outside the family, at a day school, in the park, or in a similar situation, the parents typically feel great anger at the person responsible and feel great guilt for having placed their child in those circumstances.

In this situation, counseling is probably necessary to determine if the parents really were negligent. Did they "set up" their child by not paying enough attention to where their child was and what was happening to him or her, or would the situation have happened regardless? It's perfectly possible for caring, attentive parents to have a terrible random incident such as an outside molestation take place. They have to work through the pain and come to terms with what fate has dealt them.

For our purposes, however, we are going to be concerned with molestation within the family. What happens to one parent when the other molests a child?

Sheila

Sheila had what she thought was a warm relationship with her husband and her two energetic and lovely girls. She tried to provide balanced family activities and a very traditional family environment. However, she had a blind side. Without her knowing it, her husband had been molesting one of her daughters from the age of three or four until the girl was eleven.

Sheila found out by coming home early from shopping one day and walking in on her husband and daughter.

Staying with the Pain

Sheila had multiple emotions. She was angry, perhaps angrier than she had ever been before. She was also devastated, as though her entire support system had been kicked away from beneath her. She felt the pain of her child.

And she felt guilt. How could she not know? The only answer Sheila could find was that she simply didn't. Her husband was extremely discreet, doing it only when she was away. The girl, who always seemed sort of sad and droopy, never said anything. Later, the girl told her that her father said all daddies love their little girls that way and told her other lies to keep her from talking to Sheila about it.

Most of all, Sheila was confused. What was she to do now?

Sheila and her husband called in the grandparents for consultation and help. The husband's family, naturally enough, wanted to protect him. They insisted that she keep everything hush-hush "for the good of the children." They said the last thing that should happen was any kind of a scandal. It would ruin not only their son and Sheila, but would mark the children for life.

At first Sheila tried to accept what they were saying. But she found she could no longer live with her husband. Eventually she decided that the only course open to her was to be strong for herself and the girls in a way she believed was right. She insisted he move out.

Almost immediately the ridiculing from his family began. They called her a hypocrite and said a good wife would stand up for her husband no matter what the trouble was. They made Sheila feel somehow responsible and guilty for asking her husband to leave and for taking his children from him, even though she knew she didn't dare let him have them.

Although she was determined to make it on her own, she felt guilt at every turn. Her actions, as a result, were not strong and purposeful. She stopped disciplining the children and in general became an ineffective parent. She began to let the girls get away with coming in late and not doing chores in order to make up for her imagined sins. When they asked questions about what was happening, she couldn't answer. Feeling as if she should have known, she was too guilt-ridden to be of much help to the girls. They all began to be less defined as persons . . . and less secure.

Sheila's husband persuaded her to settle out of court. He said that going to court would only hurt the children.

Sheila began to feel that if she went to court, somehow she would be to blame for any problems the children got into later on. Besides, she felt sorry for her husband. Even though she now realized that a part of him had always been a stranger to her, she still could not help but be sympathetic to the low state he had gotten himself into.

Feeling confused and hurt, she agreed to child support, half the house when the kids turned eighteen, and no alimony, even though she had never worked before. In her hurt her attitude became, "I can make it on my own. I don't need a husband to support me."

The Harsh Economic Realities

It was, of course, foolish bravado on her part. Sheila had been trained as a secretary when she was in high school, but was so out of touch with the marketplace that she didn't realize that she couldn't make a fourth the amount her husband, a professional, could bring home.

Almost immediately she faced a financial crisis. The family was reduced to living almost at the poverty level. Even if she worked at two or three jobs, she couldn't make enough money to provide those things for her daughters that she felt all children should have. Just keeping up the house, the appliances, the yard and car, finding money for shopping— let alone for leisure activities—was a terrible burden.

Sheila felt that the financial setback was her fault. She had failed to take adequate steps to provide for the family. So she added the money problems to the guilt she already felt toward the daughter who was molested as well as, incredibly, the guilt she felt toward her husband for somehow not understanding and supporting him so the tragedy wouldn't have happened.

When Sheila finally came in for therapy she was almost destitute both financially and emotionally.

GETTING WELL

Sheila's therapy consisted of reeducation. She had to realize that she and her daughters were the victims, not the culprits. She had to learn that she was not guilty for her husband's actions or for the thoughts of his family.

It was a difficult reawakening for her. She had to forgive herself for not knowing. She came to realize that given the circumstances, very few wives would have figured it out.

She had to forgive herself for her husband's actions. She came to accept that he was his own person and responsible for himself. He had done it, not her.

She had to forgive herself for what society thought about her. It was not her fault that the culture was set up to condemn both parents in cases like this, or that some people expected her to stay in the marriage no matter what.

In the end, she saw that she was a good person and a loving mother. She saw that her daughters were doing well, although they both still had to struggle with their feelings of guilt and anger over what had happened.

THE LESSON TO BE LEARNED

For those parents who have had to live through a similar situation the lesson is clear. You have to decide sooner or later whether you were the victim or the culprit. If you were the culprit, then you will have your own special hell to contend with.

But if you were the victim, then you have to be strong enough to forgive yourself. The truth is that sometimes no matter how careful you are, no matter what preventive actions you take, tragedy can strike. That doesn't mean you're to blame.

Although she was confused, Sheila was, in truth, a strong woman. She had the strength to divorce her husband and clean up an intolerable situation. Irma, on the other hand, did not have that strength.

Irma

Irma had three children, two girls, aged seven and twelve, and a younger boy. Unknown to her, her husband had been molesting the older girl for nearly six years.

It all came into the open when the girl complained of bruises in her pelvic area. She said she had been riding her bike and had crashed it.

Irma took the girl to the family doctor. The doctor was immediately suspicious and, in coordination with another physician, undertook a rigorous physical exam. Laboratory tests revealed semen in the girl's vagina.

When the doctor called in a social worker and presented the problem to the family, Irma was speechless. But not her husband. He verbally assailed the doctor, saying the doctor had no right to conduct the exam without the specific permission of the parents. In addition, her husband said the lab tests must be flawed, something the doctor said was highly unlikely, but technically possible. Somehow, it had become the doctor's fault.

Irma was confused. On the one hand there was the damning evidence. On the other was the denial from her husband and his accusations against the doctor. The girl, frightened, denied anything had happened to her and maintained the story about the biking accident.

Irma suspected the worst was really the truth. And like Sheila, quickly realized the alternatives. She could break up the family to protect the children. But if she did, she would be admitting the worst had indeed happened. She would be admitting she hadn't known her child was being molested. She would feel guilty for the molestation, even for not understanding her husband better.

Her husband was obviously frightened. He told her she had to support him. In the end Irma, more afraid of the guilt she would feel if she admitted what had happened, gave in. She went along with her husband. It was all the doctor's fault. Her husband was innocent. The family would continue on as before.

But what of the little girl? She certainly knew the truth. And eventually, one way or another, she would have to deal with it.

DENIAL

As difficult as it may be to deal with misplaced feelings of guilt that come about because of child molesting, how much sadder it is when the truth is denied. Down deep Irma certainly knew the truth ... or suspected it. How long could she and her daughter keep it bottled up? How long before one or the other finally let it break out into the open? And until then, Irma would truly be guilty of forcing her daughter to remain in what could only charitably be described as a bad family situation.

The best way of dealing with it remains to get the truth out and then deal with any guilt. Covering up only compounds the problem.

Get help from your priest, rabbi, or minister as well as a psychologist. Check out the groups and services at hospitals, mental health facilities, and child welfare organizations in your community.

Use the experts and resources as possibilities. Remember that child molesting is a disease that can be cured. It is many times a legacy from generation to generation. Stop it now and help all the people involved by being knowledgeable and informed.

PART 2

Five Ways Teens Misbehave

As we saw in Part I, children have many different causes for their behavior—from biological problems to sibling rivalry, from peer pressure to having working or divorced parents.

Now we'll see that there are as many different types of problem behavior as there are reasons for it. Some teenagers are rebellious, some abusive toward their parents. Others refuse to take on responsibility or bully everyone around them.

In Part II, we'll take a close look at each type of behavior and teach you how to recognize patterns in your teen's actions. We'll show you how feelings of guilt may have hampered your ability to cope with these behaviors and how guilt-proof parents handle these same situations.

10
The Abusive Teen

We've learned that children don't normally see that their parents get hurt and feel pain. When they do see it, they tend not to empathize. For teenagers, what's important is immediate gratification—getting what they want when they want it.

When teenagers *don't* get what they want, they may take out their frustrations on their parents and may even blame their parents. In the midst of their narcissism, their actions toward their parents can be brutal. Unfortunately, most loving parents simply don't recognize the behavior for what it is—abuse.

You may cringe at the word *abuse*. It sounds strong, but abuse means behavior that takes advantage of someone to achieve a selfish end. And because teens are naturally self-centered, they often act abusively, hitting parents at their weakest points. That doesn't mean teens are innately bad—with your love and guidance, they'll learn not to be abusive—but denying that their actions do take advantage of you won't help either of you deal with them.

Loving parents deny abuse because of their unrealistic notion of children. They think that they are entitled to and should be receiving love in return, so when the child doesn't give back love, they dismiss the behavior as temporary, due to a "bad day," the child not feeling well, or other explanations.

The denial just complicates matters. When teens treat their parents badly, parents naturally feel angry. But if they deny their children's bad behavior, they may turn that anger into guilt—after all, who would be angry at a child who's not misbehaving?

The way out of this quagmire is recognition. If parents begin to recognize bad behavior as abusive, then the whole pattern of illogical thinking can come to a halt. If they see that they're being abused, even if it's by their children, they will begin to realize that there's nothing wrong in feeling angry about it.

Recognizing abusive behavior and the fact that you're angry about it are the first steps toward stopping it.

The primary goal of this chapter is to help you build that awareness. It suggests solutions along the way and there will be more solutions later in the book. Most parents are like boxers in a ring who don't realize that there's a fight going on. While their opponent is pummeling them, they are trying to read the evening paper.

So let's begin. Does your child abuse you? Do you recognize it when it happens? Here are some very real and often too frequent instances. You may be very surprised to at last understand some behavior that you've witnessed, but couldn't figure out.

TYPES OF ABUSIVE BEHAVIOR

1. Circular Behavior

This is a situation that no matter what you do, you can't seem to correct bad behavior. The child continually tries to undermine you by never letting an agreement between the two of you culminate.

You set up a very clear contract with the child. Every day when he gets home from school, he's to empty the dishwasher. He can go out only *after* the dishwasher has been emptied.

However, when you come home, the dishwasher hasn't been emptied and he's out. Or the dishwasher has been half emptied. Or the door of the dishwasher is open and your son protests, "I was just getting ready to empty it when you showed up!"

Circular behavior is where teens don't do what they are supposed to do, or they just do it a little and you end up being continually angry at them. But you can't quite pin them down.

Circular behavior is a kind of power play. They want what they want. Nobody wants to stay home and wash dishes. So a teen may cleverly try 25 or 100 different ways of getting out of it instead of settling down and simply doing it.

People who see the situation will very often misinterpret it. Some will say it's because the parents are not being consistent. But as a parent, you know that you can be consistent, consistent, and consistent, yet the child will still not do what he is supposed to do. The minute you turn your back, the child's shirking his duties again.

The narcissistic teen will take full advantage of any opportunity to get out of his responsibilities. This may take the form of not emptying the dishwasher no matter what. His whole energy is now aimed at *not* doing this job.

The child becomes a formidable opponent. Children have a lot of energy. You have to go to work, clean the house, pay attention to other things. They have lots of free time to devote to getting out of doing the dishwasher at 6 o'clock. And that's what they'll do.

The child does not see that the reason you want the dishes emptied is to make it easier for you when you already have so many other things to do. The child simply wants her or his way.

One of the things that undermines parents is when people say, "Oh that's just kids, forget it." You start to believe that it's just the way kids act and back away from insisting on performance. Remember that part of your unwritten contract as a parent is to teach your children to be responsible adults. Don't always listen to well-meaning people who tell you to forget it. Backing away is not usually the right answer.

2. Name Calling

This can be subtle. After all, if they use a four-letter word, they know they'll probably get in major trouble.

One child at seven called her mother "Mommy Dearest" after the movie of the same name with all its negative implications. Another might make innuendoes that you're a little overweight, particularly just as you've finished dressing to go out. Yet another might make critical comments to you that you can't really discipline for because they are fleeting or sniping (done on the run!).

The tendency is to dismiss it all as childish behavior. It is indeed childish, but it's also abusive. It's abusive because they know that it gets to you and they do it for that reason.

Don't think that children don't know "where you live." They know exactly where your weaknesses are. So when they want something—because of their inexperience they have little conscience about it—some will go for that weakness and whittle away until they get what they want. Often parents don't realize that they are smart enough or manipulative enough to be doing those things on purpose. But think again. They just might be!

3. Guilt Trips

Parents are always told they lay guilt trips on their children. But as a parent, you know it's a two-way street. Kids can deliver a guilt-trip whammy that really hurts.

"Everyone else has a ten-speed bicycle and I want one, too!"

You know you shouldn't feel guilty. But then you look around and see that in the crowd your child runs with, the other parents have indeed bought the children all the same kind of bike or the same kind of tennis shoes or the same something. Everyone has one except your child. Because your kid is being left out, you feel guilty.

Of course, guilt-tripping doesn't necessarily have to be limited to objects. "Mom, everybody else's parents have volunteered to go on a field trip. You've gotta take me!"

You can't go because you have to work and therefore your child can't go either. That's a double whammy guilt trip. It's those times when you have to choose yourself over them because of circumstances or because of monetary considerations that they can really make you feel guilty. You don't want to hurt them and you're angry with yourself because you can't be everything for them all the time.

So you're the perfect candidate for a guilt trip. Even if the child applies only the slightest pressure, you're filled with remorse. It hurts to know it's your fault that your child is missing out.

4. Comparisons

"You did more for my brother than you did for me."

Children have great memories for this. And they don't play

fair. When they make comparisons, they don't say something like, "Dad or mom, sit down because I want to talk to you about this. . . ."

Instead they blindside you while you're thinking about something else and thrust out fifteen comparisons about how Johnny at this age got so and so. They choose a time when you're tired, occupied with something else, and don't have it together enough to sit down and remember the way it really was. Your first reaction is to believe the child and try to even things out. So you sort of say, "Is that right? Well, maybe that is so." And you go along with what the child really wants. It's only later on that you think of all the reasons not to.

But it's too late. Usually, after you've given in, you're reluctant to go back on your decision no matter how unfairly you've been battered because you're afraid of not keeping your word or being labeled inconsistent.

Comparisons are very effective methods of parent abuse, particularly for children who have good timing.

5. Triangles

As we saw earlier, divorced parents are particularly susceptible to triangles, but they can happen in any family. The children deliberately set mom and dad against each other.

In one case, a father disciplined by raising his voice when the children did something wrong. Later, when the mother got home from work, the youngest child ran to her and said, "Dad yelled at me. He really screamed."

The mother, who had read a lot about child abuse and was on the lookout for even a hint of it, was immediately outraged that the father had yelled at the children. The father now had to defend his actions in front of the children, who enjoyed the show.

In another family, where two divorced parents remarried and brought their children together, triangles were common. When little Jane was there for the first time, she told her dad that her new stepmom offered her a cigarette. Her dad got really angry with mom for that.

The truth was that there was an older child who did smoke and the mom did let him have a cigarette. Jane, however, saw that as an opportunity to set dad against stepmom in order to get her way and deliberately set up a little triangle.

Children who want to abuse parents set up triangles to make one parent look good and the other look bad. All that they really want, however, is their way.

Watch out for these set-ups. Parents must be a team. Talk to each other as much as possible. Check out each other's situations as often as possible, particularly when things seem to be escalating into negative feelings. When parents don't communicate, it feeds triangles. This is particularly true with families where both parents work and there is little time to check out each situation.

The best you can do is to continually be aware of triangles in a family and guard against them, given the limited amount of time you have available, your tiredness, and the fact that you're not always perfect.

6. Blackmail

Your child knows that it's really important to you that she behave because you're having your boss over to dinner. Suddenly she starts acting sullen and disrespectful. You panic. You can't have your boss thinking that's the kind of child you raise. So she lets you buy her off. She'll be friendly and courteous *if* you'll let her go to that concert next week.

Or your son knows that it's important to you that he get good grades. But instead of studying to get the grades, he goofs off. When you complain, he lets you buy him off with an allowance bonus for studying.

Again because children don't have experience, they don't know how important it is to get along with a boss or understand the long-term value of getting good grades. They just know that they had other plans for dinner or that studying is hard work. After all, so far in their lives they've been able to affect the world around them so that everything always works out for them.

What they *do* understand is that if something is important to you, you'll be willing to do almost anything to make it happen. That's when they start demanding a ransom in return.

7. Not Living Up to Agreements

This is when you continually try to live up to your bargains with them, while they consistently don't live up to theirs with you. Even when you write out a contract with them, they don't live up to it.

For example, the agreement may be that they would be in bed every night by ten without you having to nag them. But they only do it three out of five nights and come up with all types of excuses to soften you. Their homework isn't finished, their best friend had a bad day and they had to console her on the phone, or whatever.

But accepting excuses for a broken agreement isn't a two-way street. If you tell them you can't take them to the movie after all because you have to work, they do not usually understand and may feel that you have let them down again. The "again" may only be two times a month and not the 40 percent of each week that they do not come through on their agreements, but somehow your excuses do not seem as important to them as theirs are supposed to be to you.

It is tough. Most parents don't feel they should get at their child's level and say, "Listen, you didn't live up to your end so I'm not going to live up to mine." They don't want to be petty.

On the other hand, you're frustrated. You had an agreement; they broke it. Why?

The reason is that they're self-centered and resent any kind of restrictions. They should be allowed to do anything they want whenever they want.

Breaking an agreement with you gets even for your insistence on limiting them in the first place. When they break the agreement they are saying in essence, "See how powerful I am?

See how weak you are?"

So what can you do? One simplistic solution that may work is to actually get down on their level. Maybe you should stop taking the high road. If you don't keep your agreements with them occasionally, it will show them how it feels. If they cannot take the trash outside without a harangue, then maybe you will not be able to drive them to the soccer game on Saturday.

You want them to see that you are a person too, not a servant. You want them to feel how it feels when someone doesn't come through for them. Maybe it isn't petty behavior. Maybe it's reality, because who else but you would keep rewarding them over and over again in the face of disrespect and irresponsible behavior?

8. Feigning Illness

Some children get their way by pretending to be sick. Earlier, we learned about a child who put hot water in his mouth to fake a high temperature. Another would get ill so she didn't have to go to school in the morning and then get well around eleven o'clock, when the class she hated was over. Her mother, wanting to be loving and caring, would take off work at eleven and come home every day to take her to school.

Feigning illness is a way to abuse someone who cares about you. It's using that person's love as a weapon. If you're a caring parent and you think your child is sick, you'll start taking him to doctors, start changing your time schedule, start running around taking care of him.

Teens know that it causes problems with your schedule and makes life difficult for you. They know they are inconveniencing you. Worst of all, they really might not care. Narcissism makes the child believe that the only thing that's important is getting out of the test she hasn't studied for or not having to see the girlfriend he just broke up with. Abusing you may be one way of accomplishing that.

We know of one parent who finally said, "You're going to school on Monday or you're going to the hospital. If you are that sick, let's get you admitted and cured." The child went to school.

9. Taking Advantage When You're Weak

Sometimes children wait until you're on the phone to ask you for things. Sometimes they make demands on you when you're sick or very, very tired.

In one case a divorced woman took her three children to Europe for a wonderful vacation. When they got back, she found her business partner had run out with all her money. She had to work eighteen hours a day to try to save her business.

She was living in a beautiful home with the children, who previously had been well behaved. But now they started acting up because they wanted to have the freedom they had had when on vacation.

The mother tried to clamp down. She grounded them. But they would sneak out and bring friends in through the window and have parties. What with work and the kids, the mother's stress level rose and she was hospitalized for exhaustion. So she called the dad up and he came and got them.

He had previously been treated for ulcers and was trying to avoid stress. He had them for two weeks and then called and told the mom that she had to come and take them back. He said, "I can't control them, they've never been this way before." As soon as she went and got them, he readmitted himself to the hospital with bleeding ulcers.

The kids weren't psychologically sick. They were just narcissistic. They wanted their own way. In therapy they later admitted, "We were really angry with Mom because she tried to tie us down and then sent us over to Dad's to live."

These were essentially good children. They wanted their freedom and were simply taking advantage when their parents were down to try to get it.

10. Refusing to Socialize

You talk to your kids and say it's so important to Grandma and Grandpa for them to come out and say hello while they're visiting. The kids stay in their rooms.

They know this hurts your feelings and their grandparents' feelings because it shows they don't care. It shows that lying around their rooms or watching TV or whatever is more important than being with the family.

Or perhaps they don't talk to your friends when your friends come in. They run away or growl at them or whatever.

It's not that you expect them to carry on a lengthy conversation. You've taught them all the manners in the world, and now they do this. It's as though they don't care about anybody else in the house but themselves.

No, it's not just childish behavior to be quickly excused. It's deliberate abusive behavior. They are getting you for some frustration they are feeling either with you or with the rest of the world.

You don't deserve such treatment. It's important to deal with this behavior even if you have to take a difficult and embarrassing stand in front of the relatives or friends. Until you deal with it, you can't feel good about yourself or them.

11. Borrowing and Not Returning

One parent reported that his son borrowed $20 from his friends. Then the boy rushed in and demanded that the parent loan him $20. It was urgent, a matter of life and death.

The loving parent obliged. The son took the $20 and paid back his friends, but never bothered to repay the parent. (It really shows who's important!)

Remember, to the teen, the parent can be strictly a provider. The teen may not even think of the shirt he borrowed or the necklace you loaned as something to be returned. If it's yours, they think it's theirs.

It's up to you to help your child see you as a person. But don't expect this to be an easy task.

You can begin by letting your child know you have limitations. You get tired, you can run out of money or patience. You have certain things that belong to you that he cannot use. Do not always be available for her every need and whim. Above all else, say, "No. I'm a person, too, and I do not always want to loan you my things. I love you, but I will not *always* share my time, space, and money with you. Maybe another time, but not now. Thank you for understanding."

12. "I Want to Live with You, but Never Have Any Rules"

Even though teens know they need their parents economically, they often act like they're doing the parents a favor to live in their home. They'll stay, but they won't tolerate being tied down by rules.

Mom says that she is to be in by ten o'clock. She says, "That's it, Mom. I don't want to hear any more about it. Just turn it off." And she storms out of the room swearing under her breath.

The mom is intimidated. Is this her daughter? She's now a teenager and growing up. Is this the kind of adult she's going to become? Is living here really so miserable for her? The mother goes into the corner, sits down, and feels terrible guilt.

There's nothing to be guilty about, however. The teenager is preparing for the day when he or she will set their own rules by testing the limits of yours.

Somewhere deep inside the teen knows she does have a good deal going. She's just pushing to see how much freedom she can get. It's up to you to give her responsibility as she is ready for it, and to refuse her freedom when she's not.

13. Never Saying Thank You

You've just spent an hour and a half in the kitchen making a wonderful dinner for them. They come in, take one bite, and say, "Ugh, what is this? We've never had this stuff before. It's terrible." Then they go get hot dogs or pizza.

You feel bad, for yourself . . . and for them. You didn't expect overwhelming gratitude, but a decent "thank you" would have been nice. And what kind of people are they who have such a bad attitude? What have you raised?

You've raised a teenager. And you've just experienced yet another form of parent abuse.

Before you can combat your child's lack of appreciation, you must first combat its effect on your self-image. You should realize your worth as a parent and person. Think how lucky your child is to have you. Join a group of other parents to talk about this. Get an objective opinion from someone who has had children and understands the dynamics of everyday interactions with teens. Try to write down what occurred and see how it made you feel.

Then you'll be able to teach your kids to show gratitude. Let them see how indignant you are that you, who loves, provides, and cares for them, is treated so badly. That way, you can deal with your angry feelings by expressing them constructively and not swallowing them.

BUT IS IT REALLY ABUSE?

That's the nagging question. Are the children really being abusive or are they "just being children?" That's the question that robs parents of their strength and their will to do something about it.

Parenting is such a difficult, complex thing. It's like walking on soft noodles. You're never sure of your footing. You're never sure your perception of what's happening is right. How do you know it's really parent abuse?

Here is a simple test that you can apply *to every situation* when you even suspect that your children are abusing you.

Momentarily leave the situation. Get out of the room, the car, or the house and get where you can think clearly. Now ask yourself this simple question:

"Would I let anybody else do this to me?"

If the answer is yes, then chances are it's not parent abuse. On the other hand, if the answer is no, then it probably *is* parent abuse.

If it's a kind of behavior that you wouldn't let a spouse, a friend, an employer, or anyone else get away with, then you're probably being abused.

LEARNING TO COPE

This chapter is intended to make you aware that there's a force out there who wants to have its way and doesn't understand (or maybe even care) that you have needs, too.

Becoming aware that their teens are often abusive can make parents feel like they've failed, that it's too late to change their kids. But it's definitely not too late.

First, try to recognize yourself in your children. Didn't you act in a similar way to your parents? If not, didn't some of your friends? Didn't they ultimately turn out all right? As soon as you do this, you can get past that hopeless feeling that comes from realizing your child acts abusively.

Also, remember that this behavior is part of your child's growing-up process and separating from you, as well as trying to make his or her way in the world.

It is just the way things are. In general this behavior can be expected. If parents teach their children from a very early age to share with others, to be responsible for their actions, and to treat their parents with respect and see them as people who have limited amounts of time, patience, money, and energy, then a child's selfishness can be curbed. But it is almost never erased completely.

If you are confronted with abuse, then as soon as you see it for what it is and admit that you are angry about it, you can start doing something to change the situation. Remember, your child does not always have your best interests at heart. But that's all right, as long as you realize it, understand it, and start to balance the equation.

You are the parent and you have the right to be happy and free from guilt. Believe it and it will start to happen. This is a process, a long one, but one that will end.

11

The Rebellious Teen

For most people, the word *rebellion* is almost synonymous with the word *teenager.* Virtually every teenager rebels in some way—by talking back, refusing to do what parents want, rejecting the parents' religion, dressing in styles parents don't approve of, or listening to music they don't like.

A certain amount of rebellion is necessary for teenagers to establish their independence. But if teenagers take rebellion too far or if their parents don't know how to handle it, the conflict between parent and teen can cause permanent damage to their relationship.

141

PSYCHOLOGICAL REBELLION

We all know teenagers who are always ready to argue with whatever anyone says. A mother tells her daughter to go to sleep because it's late, and the daughter says, "Gees, Mom. I'm not tired. Get off my back. I'm old enough to make my own decisions!"

Another parent says it's time to do homework. The son replies, "No, it's not. I'll do it later. It's *my* homework, not yours."

An adult says it's a lovely day, the sun is shining, and the birds are singing. The teenager looks out the window and says, "You've got to be kidding. I hate this weather."

Get the picture? Whatever you say, the teenager says the opposite.

Trying to Get Heard

If as a parent you took this kind of behavior personally, you'd go crazy. So you ignore it, but it still eats away at you. You can't help but wonder if every interaction has to be this continuous struggle.

Adults are used to having intelligent, considerate conversations with people. More important to us, we are used to having our opinions respected, our judgment validated at least occasionally. But if your child is psychologically rebellious, it's a fight from the first breath you draw in the morning.

No matter what you say, the child's opinion, often expressed very forcefully, is the opposite. It's as if everything you value is up for grabs.

Because you're a loving parent, you try to adjust. You say

such things as, "All people are entitled to an opinion. You're a person so you're entitled to yours. But I'm a person, too, so I'm entitled to my own. Let's just agree to disagree." Doesn't this sound mentally healthy and sane? Wrong!

You may think it's a perfectly generous offer on your part. After all, you probably don't always think the kid's opinion is valid or logical, but you're ready to bend over backwards to be fair. What could be fairer than offering to simply accept the child's right to have an opinion if she'll accept yours?

Only a child like this really isn't interested in being fair or, for that matter, in listening to what you have to say on any subject. She only *seems* to listen, waiting impatiently for a break in the conversation when she can contradict you.

If you complain to your friends, they're likely to say, "She's just being a kid. They all act contrary at that age." The trouble, of course, is that you have to live with it. And the cumulative effect of constantly being contradicted in your own house can be frustrating and stressful . . . to the point where you finally blow up, making a spectacle of yourself and reinforcing the kid's opinion that you're a blithering idiot.

Eventually, you may explode and shout something like, "Stop telling me whatever I say is wrong. Stop contradicting!" Then for good measure you add, "I've been around twenty years longer than you. I work forty hours a week to support you. I've seen life and know what's what. I've paid my dues. How dare you contradict *anything* I say!"

Of course the child assumes a hurt expression during your fit, which changes to sarcasm as you finish. He may then grunt in reply or simply walk out of the room as if you weren't even there. At which you sputter and rage ineffectually.

So who looks like the fool? You do. If this happened only once a year, you might be able to live with it. But when it starts to happen more often as you get tired of the no-win situation with the rebellious child, you begin to ask if there isn't a better way.

THE BENEFITS OF REBELLION

A certain amount of psychological rebellion is good. After all, you want your teenagers to be independent adults. For thirteen or more years, you've seen them as kids. You've told them what they should do, suggested where they should do it and probably when. Now they are only trying to assert themselves and show that they are your equals. This is bound to grate on you because many of their statements are immature. You aren't used to your kids expressing opinions of their own with such vehemence.

This behavior is all the more difficult because it comes on suddenly. One night they go to sleep agreeing with you and the next morning they wake up raging maniacs. Dr. deGarcia recalls kissing her daughter good night and then having her wake up the next morning saying, "I hate you. I want to move out and live with my friends."

Dr. deGarcia knew that this was the beginning of her daughter's separation from the family. It could be a rough ride to her independence or it could be a little less bumpy, depending on how the child reacted to continued discipline and direction and how her mom reacted to the emotional changes of her daughter. It also depended on her mom's ability not to take the rebellion personally, but to see it as a stage to go through to get to the other side of adulthood for her child.

PAYING ATTENTION

When kids act rebellious, you do have to pay attention. For one thing, they're big now, frequently bigger than you are. For another, they have freedom. If they don't like the way you respond, they can always walk out the door. Also, you don't want to alienate them or they won't come to you with their problems.

But you find yourself left out of their lives. They no longer think you deserve respect simply because you're their parent, so they discount your advice and experience. At the same time, they expect you to listen to all their opinions, even when their opinion is simply the opposite of whatever yours is.

Naturally, this is going to be difficult, particularly for the parent who has tried to listen in the past to the child's opinions, but now finds the tone of voice and attitude trying. This adjustment can be painful particularly if the parents haven't yet started seeing their kids as young adults, but still long for the little child of the past.

It's helpful to remember, however, that chances are the child is bumping up against the real world in lots of places and taking quite a few scrapes and bruises. This can be very frustrating. What she or he is looking for at home is a place where the world is under control.

Faced with the reality that he or she knows very little about the world outside, at the home the child seeks to dominate the environment by spouting off like a world-master authority on every conceivable subject. As Dr. deGarcia's father says, "They're talking just to hear their heads rattle." Of course the child needs someone to listen and that someone usually ends up being the parent. If you resist, they will sometimes retreat to their rooms and that's bad, too.

HOW MUCH SHOULD YOU TOLERATE?

The key is to let teens know how inconsiderate they are without breaking their spirit or going into incoherent raging fits. Many parents just give up. They listen to their children's know-it-all opinions, and don't try to contradict them.

One role parents must never assume is that of willing victim. You must strive to be aware of manipulation by your children. No matter how much you love them, make the effort to stay out of their psychological games.

Unfortunately, this is easier said than done. It requires that you not fall into the trap of becoming too emotional when dealing with the teen.

If you work at being ruled less by your emotions each time your child wants his or her way, you probably will discover that soon the teen is treating you a bit more respectfully and talking to you as if you actually had brains.

Much contrary behavior on the part of teenagers will occur in brief episodes. It'll last a week or two, then abate only to return a few weeks or even a month or two later.

Simply being detached emotionally, understanding where it's coming from, and realizing that the teenage years are not the time to make a final judgment about the value of this person can be helpful. Remember that your child will try on many personality roles during this time. If you push too hard, he or she might just get stuck in this one (God forbid!). Sometimes parents who ignore some, correct a little, but who avoid direct and angry confrontations can work with the child with only minimal problems.

You can sometimes cut down on psychological rebellion by pointing it out. "Are you aware, son, that you have contradicted the last five statements I've made? Do you really have contrary opinions or are you only saying the opposite of what I say to hurt me?" This may only add fuel to the fire, but pointing out inappropriate behavior does take energy away from it, even for the child that continues to use it.

Letting the teenager know you're aware of the nature of the behavior may give him cause to rethink and reposition and give you at least a temporary respite. (This usually happens after the teen has left the room in a huff.)

THE REBELLIOUS PERSONALITY

The rebellion we've discussed so far in this chapter is psychological rebellion—where the teenager challenges the parent's authority verbally and asserts his or her independence through know-it-all pontificating. Almost all teenagers rebel this way.

But there is another type of rebellion that can be more intense. This is the rebellious personality—the independent or headstrong child who becomes strongly rebellious in the teen years.

The child's predisposition toward rebellion may not be obvious early in life, since he or she doesn't have the power to act on those feelings, so parents are unable to handle the rebellion properly. This can lead to what seems like a surprisingly intense rebellious streak in the teenager. The rebellious personality, coupled with the normal rebellion of the teen years, suddenly gets the teenager into trouble at school, at home, virtually everywhere.

If the rebellious personality isn't handled properly, it can develop into a serious problem requiring counseling. The rebelliousness can become severe or neurotic (which is defined as continued illogical or immature behavior at inappropriate times).

Mike

Mike was fifteen years old. He had been a nice, well-behaved boy all his life. Now suddenly he was failing badly at school. He was not turning in his homework, and not finishing his tests; worst of all, he was back-talking some of his teachers resulting in Saturday morning detentions.

His parents were saddened. At home he used foul language and his sense of humor became vicious and sadistic, resulting in his continually hurting people's feelings. When his parents tried to correct him, he would not let them finish a sentence. No matter what they tried to say, he would interrupt (often raising his voice) with a denial or a contradictory opinion. They felt, with some justification, that he was out of control. What was worse, they had no idea why he was acting the way he was or what they could do about it.

When Mike drove his mother to tears, his father, who never even stepped on ants, got so furious that he backhanded him. The result was the man only felt ashamed of himself. Mike displayed indignation and acted appalled at his father's actions, forgetting that he had caused it all.

THE EARLY YEARS

As it turned out, Mike had a psychologically rebellious personality. It was his nature to be rebellious.

As a child, virtually from birth, he had shown an independent streak. He liked to play by himself, to do things on his own. At school he had basically been a loner. His parents left him to unfold psychologically. They felt that it was okay for him to be different.

His mother realized he had the right to live his own life but she also wanted him to have many friends. In her frustration, she would sometimes say, "Go out and play with Danny," "Leroy just called, call him back," or "Tomorrow I'm signing you up for soccer and you're going to play on the team whether you like it or not!"

These, of course, are double messages. But they are not enough, by themselves, to cause a kid serious problems. You want the best for your children, so there are times when voicing your concerns is best, even if those concerns contradict other messages you've given them.

The trouble was the mother was not a good fit with her son. Her personality was achievement oriented. She felt more comfortable when Mike was gregarious and achieved. She felt frustrated when he was withdrawn or moody.

She coped better than most. She really loved him and tried to accept his "loner" personality, but it still hurt her to see him at school parties, sitting quietly with a distant sad look in his eyes, even though he constantly protested, "I don't care." So she tried to tactfully change him.

When her subtle suggestions failed, Mike's mother found his loner stance increasingly hard to bear. As Mike did not fulfill her expectations, she was less able to openly be warm toward him. And this made her feel guilty. So she badgered him more and more to have a "popular" personality or at least try not to be antisocial.

At an early stage, Mike sought help from his dad. Dad was warm and supportive, but if there was a problem, he assumed that Mike was giving his mom a hard time and insisted that Mike follow through on whatever his mom wanted.

So from Mike's perspective, there were only two alternatives. On the one hand he could give in, try to become the person she wanted him to be. This would mean, however, that he'd have to give up his own personality, a thing which he instinctively did not want to do and probably could not do.

The other alternative was to rebel. To refuse to do what his mother wanted. If he rebelled against his mother's pushing then he would be able to preserve his own personality. This was the course he chose. From his earliest days, whenever she would want him to do something, he would automatically try to do the opposite.

Of course, he was little and she was all powerful. He could not come out and simply say, "No. I won't eat the custard." But he could eat only part of it. And throw part of it on the floor. And maybe smear part of it under the table top.

He could be subtly rebellious in ways his mom probably didn't understand or wouldn't punish him for. And that's what he did, for almost all his young life.

Of course, at some level his mother was aware of this. She spoke of Mike as a difficult and frustrating child, one she had to work hard to like, even though she loved him. For Mike's part, he was a clever child. He learned early on that being polite could cover a whole lot of rebellion. So he was always polite and his mother could never quite put her finger on what the problem was.

Then, almost overnight, he became a teenager. He was big, strong, able to get a job, and convinced that tomorrow (or certainly by next Tuesday at the latest) he would be an adult with an adult's power. Suddenly Mike was no longer intimidated by his mom. He no longer *needed* her to be polite. For the first time he could openly get away with showing the rebellious personality he had had all along. For him it was a welcome breath of fresh air. A chance to quit hiding and act like he felt.

For his parents, particularly his mom, however, it was an unbelievable shock. This nice polite boy was suddenly terribly rebellious. No matter what mom or dad said, he said the opposite. No matter what they wanted him to do, he did the opposite. They felt as if they were seeing a totally new person, someone they didn't know. It was, of course, the same Mike. Only now he was showing his true colors.

Mike eventually did get squared away. He had to go to therapy to break his self-centeredness. It had begun to cripple him in all areas because the behavior was demonstrated to all adults, including his bosses.

At sixteen, after he had been fired from two jobs, he figured he might have a problem and it might not *all* be his mom. In fact, some of what she said now began to make sense.

Mike's behavior is not that unusual for teenagers of both genders. Many teenagers' sudden contrariness has been there all along. It's just that it didn't show up until adolescence.

WHAT TO DO

It's important to remember that something that took a young lifetime to develop isn't going to be corrected or changed overnight.

If you have a teenager who has a rebellious personality, it will undoubtedly take time to change his or her behavior. Some therapy may be necessary.

However, to start, what you must do is to become aware of what's happening. (This book will help you to do some self-counseling, but for severe cases, an outside counselor may be required.) It's important that two things be accomplished for the benefit of the teenager:

1. Preserve that rebellious personality. After all, it's the rebellion that allowed Mike to survive the bad fit with his parents, particularly his mom. It's probably his greatest strength. However, don't let the teen talk angrily to you. Call him on it if he talks to you disrespectfully.

    But if the results are a shouting match, turn on your heels and leave. Remember, it takes two. Avoid shouting matches by leaving the situation as soon as you see it coming. Then, when the child is in a quieter mood, tell him, "Whenever you raise your voice, it makes me uncomfortable. In the future when this occurs, I'll leave until we can both sit down together and talk about the issue quietly." Remember, in most cases the child wants something and if he realizes that he isn't going to be able to tell you what he wants if he shouts, he'll begin to control his voice.

2. Try to teach consideration of others by showing cause and effect. The rebellious teen needs to see others as people also. While keeping that rebellious streak in his personality, Mike has to realize how he comes across to others and how that can give others (particularly his parents) pain. What he needs to learn is how to turn his rebellious streak on or off. When his independence (his personality) is threatened, he can turn it on. But in the day-to-day course of living, he can leave it turned off and act like a warm, considerate human being. He needs to be able to control his rebellious streak so that he won't be continually obnoxious.

    A place to start is for mom to realize that Mike is not

going to hear her suggestions. She needs to teach through example. She needs to praise his strength of independence as well as criticize it. When mom realizes that it's simply a difficult fit, she can shrug off the load of guilt she's been carrying and relax. Perhaps she can even begin to explain to Mike just what the dynamics of the situation are: "Mike, we are very different. We have each other, but neither of us likes how the other goes about doing things. It will probably always be a struggle between us. But, we can learn from each other."

Mike, as do most similar teenagers, does want to succeed. Once he realizes that the avenue to it both at home and at school is to turn off the rebellious part of his personality when it's not needed, he probably will.

He needs to realize that doing it his way will probably cause a lot of trouble because he will not be able to follow directions. He'll have a hard time in life because people react angrily to defensive rebellious people.

DEALING WITH THE GUILT

As for mom, eighteen years of raising a child who is out to prove you wrong is a heavy load. She needs to find a support group. She needs to learn how to leave him alone, yet guide him without losing herself or her temper.

The key is to understand and be aware of this child's bad behavior. When it happens, leave him alone. In the classroom, if a teacher reinforces only positive behavior—studying, talking quietly, working on tasks—by walking by and touching the child lightly or tapping the desk and giving a smile of approval, and completely ignores negative behavior, the class will respond more and more positively. It is the same with your child. Reinforce good communication techniques and walk away from shouting.

The biggest problem for the parent, however, remains guilt. Somehow Mike's mom has to give up her unrealistic ideal of a "perfect, loving" baby boy and face the reality. God gave her a son, but not a son who was a perfect fit with her. She has to make the best of it.

But remember, if you and your child are a bad fit, maybe the challenge will make you stronger. In the process of trying to make it work, you will be building your own psychological muscle. You may not be able to change the fact that you and the child don't mesh that well, but you could learn an important lesson in life. Don't think of the problem as defeating. Don't feel cheated. Think positively of it as a challenge that will ultimately make a stronger and better person.

12

The Too-Smart Teen

When parents gather, the conversation frequently turns to
the children. Inevitably comparisons about intelligence begin.
My child can do this and my child can do that and so it goes.

Having a child is a blessing. Having an intelligent child is a
twin blessing, or so virtually any parent would agree. But what
most parents don't admit so readily is that the smart child can
be more difficult as well.

The reason is simply that the abusive behavior that all teens
exhibit is more sophisticated with intelligent children. As
we've seen, all children spend much of their lives making a stu-

dy of their parents. Intelligent children carry it to a fine science.

Intelligent children catch all the subtleties. They know not only which buttons to push to make their parents jump or get them what they want (something that all children understand), they also know how hard to push the buttons.

BUTTON PUSHING

For example, an intelligent child of seven or eight who wishes to get something from his mother may not take the simpler, more direct route of first asking for it (and perhaps being denied). Instead, he may begin by walking around in a sullen, dejected mood. His mother is sure to notice and when she asks, he may simply give a big sigh and look sadly away.

This is sure to pull the heartstrings of any loving mother. In a moment the young man is on her lap, being cuddled and in general bathed in affection. After a bit of encouragement, he comes forth with his problem. He doesn't really feel loved, a member of the family. He feels like he's an outsider, unwanted.

The mother is aghast. How in the world could he possibly have gotten that idea? "Of course you're loved and wanted," she responds.

He seems unconvinced and she asks suspiciously, "What makes you think you're unloved?"

If the child is really clever, he or she may hold off for a while longer. But sooner or later it's going to come out that there's a wonderful pair of roller skates in the window of the sports store that the child would love to have. All the other kids have skates . . .

The mother gives a sigh of relief. "Of course you can have skates," she responds. "Why didn't you just ask for them to begin with?"

In the early years the manipulations of the intelligent child can appear cute. The parent sees through them and is impressed and pleased with the child's precociousness. The child sees this as being rewarded for manipulative behavior and may adopt it as a standard mode of getting whatever goals he or she may have.

Troubles usually set in, however, when the child gets older and becomes so subtle and sophisticated that the parent is constantly asking, "Am I being manipulated by this gifted child or is he or she really suffering?"

Helen and Della

Guadalupe had a particularly difficult time with her two daughters, Helen and Della, when they were about to spend some time with their natural father in another city. For several weeks before the visit they were in tears, pleading not to go. They couldn't sleep nights. They told Guadalupe how much they loved her and how it would be hard to be away from her.

Their father, of course, looked forward to the visits and insisted that they come. But the mother was torn. Why were the girls behaving this way? Had something terrible happened at their father's house that they feared? What was her duty—to send them or to protect them by keeping them home?

She had read much material on child molesting and even thought that maybe the housekeeper, the gardener, anyone might be doing something. She just knew her girls were upset, but she couldn't get to the bottom of it.

The girls were bright and verbal and able to detail enough of their feelings to scare their mother without giving any real reason for it. Their mother's fear was heightened when a stepson who lived with them was critical, saying, "Why do you make them do something they obviously hate to do? How can you let them suffer like this? I'm sure glad you're not my mother!"

The mother became frantic and called her ex to explain how she felt. He was not particularly sympathetic. He criticized her for getting "sucked in" and "being so intense about everything." He said she was being used by them and everything was wonderful at his house.

So with grave reservations, she sent the girls to their father. She couldn't sleep at night through the entire week, worrying about them. She constantly had to put off the strong urge to call and see if they were all right. They had her number and if there was trouble, they had strict instructions to call her. She cleaned their rooms and prepared for the coming home party. There were no calls.

The children had a wonderful time and came back cheery and full of fun stories to retell. The mother's relief was enormous. But she began to get resentful about the ordeal that she just experienced. She asked again why they had been so upset about going.

The girls finally admitted they simply didn't want to be away from their friends for a week. They had made plans to go shopping and to do other things and they just didn't want to miss out. There had been two parties and one of the girl's boyfriends had threatened to not speak to her again if she didn't go to them.

Precious kids or monsters? One was ten, the other thirteen—what a tag team. Yet neither one realized that they had hurt their mother so badly.

These were not bad girls. They were simply young, intelligent, narcissistic adolescents. They didn't really see the pain they inflicted on their mother; they just wanted their way.

HANDLING THE TOO-SMART TEEN

Being manipulated is no fun. Intelligent children, until they begin seeing parents as people, can be ruthless at this. They want what they want when they want it and you better not get in their way.

Guadalupe would have been more effective if she had realized the girls were manipulating her. If that had been the case, she would have helped her kids see that there are limits. She could have given them less power by telling them that she trusted their dad's judgment that everything was okay. She also could have let them know that their dad would be on her side if they manipulated again.

In the future Guadalupe needs to listen to the girls, but not to always believe everything they say. She needs to tell them that she is disappointed in them, that in the future she will be more cautious about believing them. Then she should watch and interact with them enough to see that they are becoming less manipulative.

TURNING ARGUMENTS AGAINST YOU

The intelligent child frequently can turn your very arguments against you. For example, one father was at wit's end with a son who was quite smart, but who wouldn't work hard to get good grades. The father tried to use positive reinforcement, praising his son when he did well. But the boy turned the tables on his father, saying, "You only love me if I get A's."

This tactic manipulated the parents into accepting C's and D's from a student who should be getting all A's. The harder they pushed, the more he argued that their love was conditional on his grades . . . until finally they felt they had to back off.

TURNING YOU OFF

Finally, the intelligent child can simply turn off a parent whom he or she feels there are reasons for disliking. This is particularly the case with stepparents.

Gilda

Gilda had been married for a year to the father of two teenagers. She loved the father deeply and desperately wanted the marriage to work. She was determined to get the children to accept her as a loving, concerned stepparent.

One weekend the boy and girl were lounging around the house, so Gilda offered to treat them to lunch. They picked a spot and she dropped them off with $17.50 and instructions to be there in an hour when she returned to pick them up.

They thanked her profusely and told her what a great stepmom she was. But when she returned an hour later, they weren't there. They didn't show up until much later in the afternoon. It turned out that they had quickly eaten their lunch, then gone to visit their natural mother using the extra money to pay for a bus ride.

When the stepmom found out what happened, she was hurt. She felt they had used her as a free ride to their natural mom's home.

When they got home, the stepmom came unglued. What particularly galled her was their lack of concern about keeping her waiting and their willingness to openly deceive her. She yelled at them for being so thoughtless and for all their other little abuses during the previous year, such as telling her they loved her cooking, then making a gagging face to one another and throwing dinner away, or calling for a ride home, then hitching home with a friend and leaving her to hunt for them.

Both children apologized and seemed contrite. The day moved along normally and the stepmom thought that just maybe she had finally turned the corner with them.

However, the next day the boy stood her up again after calling for a ride. The girl failed to do assigned chores and then lied about having done them. They both acted rude and difficult.

The stepmom realized that both children were exceptionally bright. They were verbal and calculating. But she was torn between two responses. She felt she must accept them as they were, including their imperfections, and continue to love them regardless of what they did . . . or she had to decide that they were the enemy—callous, unconcerned, out strictly for themselves.

For Gilda, the two positions were irreconcilable. Either love her two stepchildren . . . or fight them.

She cried and cried, trying to let her new husband in on what was happening. But he simply would not believe her because his children were so different with him.

LOVE VS. CONTROL

This mom's plight is not unlike that of many other parents of intelligent, but difficult children. On the one hand the parents want to unconditionally love their children. On the other, however, they are faced with the fact that blindly accepting everything they do allows the children to let their behavior slowly deteriorate. One parent expressed it like this, "They seem to deliberately whittle away at my positive feeling until I have no choice but to cross the line [and consider them the enemy] or be a fool."

Of course, parents *never* want to see their children as the enemy. Children are their loved ones, their precious gifts. Yet, what are parents to do?

A FEW SUGGESTIONS

First, it's important to understand that letting the intelligent child psychologically manipulate you, particularly with *mean* manipulations, only feeds that child's narcissism. It only convinces the child that his or her intelligence can and should be used for selfish motivations. If the child continues with this behavior, she or he will not easily fit into the world, and will probably not find anyone else to take the stuff they dish out. You can cripple the intelligent child by allowing him or her to manipulate you.

Try to be aware and work on changing manipulative behavior. Each time you see this behavior in your child, refuse to participate in it.

Some parents do this by pointing out to the child what he or she is doing. They note the kind of manipulation, they explain that they understand what's being done, and they conclude by refusing to allow themselves to be so manipulated.

You need to let intelligent children know that they will get nothing from you except the bare necessities if they are not willing to give something back. It feels petty at first, especially if you are a mature parent, but consider the alternative. If you continue to reinforce them positively whether they are good to you or not, you hide the realities of life from them. If they do not learn to give you your due respect, they'll never give it to anyone who loves them. They will see people who love them as weak and as tools and this will destroy good relationships.

STEPS TO TAKE

First, you have to ultimately outsmart the child, something which isn't always easy. Even when you are conscious of the intelligent child's ability to manipulate you, the child can pick times when you're tired or distracted, so that often you aren't aware until later on as to how you were manipulated. So you must strive to always be alert for this.

Second, it's important to be single-minded and consistent. If you simply try to explain things logically, it turns into an intellectual game that smart kids love. Mom and dad caught on this time, so I'll be sure to be even more clever next time.

Being single-minded and consistent, particularly from an early age, does work. You may smile to yourself at the child's manipulations and take pride in his or her intelligence, but you simply don't allow yourself to be moved.

"No, you can't have the skates no matter what."

"No, I won't pick you up again if you don't wait for me this time."

"No, I won't buy you lunch next time because you didn't do as you promised this time."

You may feel that you're being petty and using playground behavior, but it does work. It teaches reality and it teaches children that they get what they give out.

Finally, you must deal with the intelligent child the same as dealing with any basically narcissistic child. You must be firm and consistent. You must not let your pride in your children's intelligence blind you to what's good for them. You must not love them so much that they become selfish, intolerable people.

A WORD ABOUT HARMING THEIR INTELLECT

Many loving parents are concerned about frustrating their intelligent children. If the child devises a complicated scheme to get what he wants and it fails, won't that be frustrating for that child? Chances are it will. It will be somewhat painful. But it will also be a lesson. It will teach the child that using his intelligence to manipulate people in a *mean* way not only doesn't work, but it hurts. The child may even learn to try openness and honesty to get what he wants. This is what you want, not intellectual war games.

As far as stifling the child's intelligence, that shouldn't be a worry as long as there are plenty of other intellectual opportunities (such as good books, advanced classes, stimulating conversations and trips, etc.). The greater danger is in feeding the narcissism. If an intellectual child gets her way over and over, the child can grow into a clinically depressed adult who is never, ever happy with anything or anyone—even herself.

The danger is not in stifling intelligence. It is in feeding narcissism.

13

The Teen Who Plays Too Much

We all know that play is important for children. Play allows them to develop character (when they play with other children) and creativity (especially when they play by themselves). Play for children, in fact, has been described as the same as work for an adult.

What we may not realize, though, is that outgrowing play as the child grows older is just as important. For example, a teenager has to choose between two alternatives—goofing off with friends or mowing the lawn. Mowing the lawn pays $10, which can later be spent on an album or some other desired item. Goofing off simply gives immediate pleasure, but satisfies no longer-term goals. What is the child to do?

Certainly children need to play. It does foster creativity, build character, and teach them about the world. But as they grow older, particularly in their teen years, they must learn that the instant gratification of play must sometimes be put off for goals that will bring even more pleasure. Thus the teenager who, as a child always chose play first, now may choose to mow the lawn to get the money for a higher goal.

But what if the teenager continues to always choose play?

Todd, Tony, and Tammy

The Martin family appeared to be all-American. Mr. and Mrs. Martin had three children, two boys and a girl. All the kids were within three years of each other and they seemed to be very happy. The parents, who had had a hard life and didn't want their children to suffer as they had, provided them with everything they wanted from money to favors ("Sure, I'll drive you to the mall whenever you want!").

When the kids reached their teen years, however, problems began to emerge. Mr. Martin operated a car dealership and detailing shop. He encouraged the boys to assist in the business, but did not demand it. He wanted them most of all to enjoy life.

The oldest boy, Todd, loved to surf. When dad told him it was time to go to work, Todd would say he would help out, but he wanted to surf first. Dad said that was okay. Soon Todd was doing nothing but surfing.

The middle son, Tony, did not want to work at the car business, which was okay with dad. But Tony needed money. So he got a job at a pizza parlor but only worked part-time hours and then only when he felt like it.

The girl, Tammy, was toying with the idea of marriage at the tender age of sixteen.

Mrs. Martin wanted all her children to at least complete high school, but they stopped attending regularly, and were constantly in trouble with the truant officer. The mother had to move them from one school to another to keep them enrolled.

Finally Todd turned eighteen. He was no longer obligated to attend school, and he dropped out. Two years later Tammy got married and quit school. Then Tony dropped out.

Both parents were dismayed. They couldn't understand why their children were unwilling to stick out school, to get steady jobs, and to wait a few years for a more mature perspective before getting married. It seemed that all the kids wanted to do was shuck their responsibilities until their personal needs were met. The parents wondered where they had gone wrong. They felt guilty for what had happened.

Looking back they recalled how they had educated the children. Each had been encouraged to pursue his or her own talents. Mrs. Martin had read many child psychology books that told her to "let the child evolve," they would finally find their head.

When things started getting rough, she put the kids in therapy and the therapist said, "Let them be. They are basically good kids and they will all turn out all right."

Both Mr. and Mrs. Martin recalled their own upbringing—tough, overbearing, uncaring, and authoritarian parents. They knew that was not the right way.

So they relied on their love of the children, child development books, and therapists. By the time they realized that was not the way either, the children had already been molded, they thought. "We did our best and we screwed up! What do we do now?" the mom said in tears.

UNDERSTANDING MATURITY

Mr. and Mrs. Martin didn't realize that by letting their children "evolve" they were allowing them to remain children, not guiding them toward responsible maturity. If they had realized that structure was important and felt less guilty about making the children work, they could have been more forceful in teaching their children that putting off pleasure until after doing a good job makes for true happiness.

We all want to love our children and see them grow up into mature adults. But sometimes, as for the Martins, love alone is not enough. We have to visualize what maturity for our children really means and then, with that goal in mind, start doing those things that will help the children reach that maturity.

Maturity can be defined in lots of different ways. But we define it like this: *Maturity is learning to put off immediate gratification so that you can achieve more important goals.*

A child plays whenever he or she feels like it. That, not just chronological age or physical size, is what makes a person a child.

A twenty-five-year-old who doesn't hold a job, who hangs out at bars, who surfs (or whatever) when he or she feels like it, is a child by this definition. Being older and bigger doesn't make a person a grown-up.

A mature person can put off immediate gratification for longer-term goals. An adult gets a job to support herself. He puts off marriage until it makes sense in "heart, head, and pocketbook." An adult doesn't have playtime until the work is done. There are many fifteen-, sixteen-, and seventeen-year-olds in America who fit this description of an adult perfectly. Again, size and age are not what makes a person mature.

The Martins encouraged their children to remain children. Since children's natural narcissism guides them to instant gratification, it takes careful, thoughtful, and consistent direction by parents to keep them from playing too much. You have to show them the benefits of patience, of waiting.

TEACHING KIDS TO WAIT

Kids very often don't realize how hard their parents work to get what they have. The kids just see the results. They don't see how the parents had to struggle through school or through apprenticeships, how they had to tolerate incompetent or abusive bosses, how they had to take jobs they didn't like, how they had to work forty-, fifty-, or sixty-hour weeks—all to provide the environment that the kids take for granted.

What parents must do is teach children the rewards of delaying immediate gratification. You must show them that maturity means sometimes sacrificing now for the future. You need to teach them that if they act in a mature way, while there may be other problems, in general they will be able to build, plan, and work toward goals that will be both for their own good as well as the good of others.

In the Martin family, the parents should have insisted that the boys work first and then get to surf or play as a reward for that work. The daughter should have been taught that marriage isn't just an easy way to get clothes, furniture, and other possessions.

Once the Martins saw what was happening, the parents did a turnaround. They stopped giving handouts. Instead, they offered to help on the condition that the children make progress (get steady jobs, work out the marriage situation—perhaps delay having children, think about returning to school, etc.). Because the Martins still had some influence on the children, they began to actively help them to mature.

Certainly for children who have already left home, it's going to be a lot harder than it would have been when the children were smaller.

On the other hand, the Martin kids had gotten out into the world. Their narcissism had bumped into reality and they were beginning to see on their own that things weren't what they had thought they were. The combination of parental guidance and reality offered the hope of eventual maturity for the kids.

CHILDREN WHO CAN'T HANDLE STRESS

Sometimes it isn't as clear as it was for the Martins. Sometimes a child seems to be taking on responsibility and handling it just fine and problems show up only in adulthood. This is the case with Jason.

Jason

Jason's parents were hard working. His mom put her husband through college and his dad then entered a profession and supported her. She stayed home with the kids until they all graduated from high school to be sure that they had discipline, support, and her time. She assigned chores to Jason and his brother. The family bought a vacation home and regularly took trips there. They attended church regularly on Sundays. Each member of the family was supportive of the others. It seemed to be the ideal all-American family again.

Alas, it wasn't to be the case. Jason was bright and successful at school and, it seemed, everywhere else. After Jason graduated from college, he acquired a high-paying job and got married. But then he became addicted to cocaine.

Jason's wife, mom and dad all pleaded with him, but to no avail. He kept his coke habit going and eventually abandoned his wife.

The family came in to Dr. deGarcia to see where they had gone wrong. But, in the course of therapy, they could find very little to fault. It seemed they had done everything right. The other child had very little to complain about how he was reared. They all felt their relationships with each other were good and wholesome. The parents felt awful and searched their memory, but couldn't come up with any clues as to what had gone wrong.

Locating the Trouble

Eventually, the parents came to realize that it was essentially Jason's personality that was at fault. From infancy, Jason had trouble handling stress. As an infant, he would get upset when relatives came over and everyone wanted to play with him. His mother unconsciously recognized this fact and tried to reduce stress at home as much as possible. At school, if he didn't do well on a test or at a sporting event, he became depressed.

However, things generally went very well for Jason. Awards, sports, and educational achievements came easy for him. Girls had always flocked to him. People really liked him. Life, he came to believe, was easy. He could do no wrong.

But after he got married and had to work at a regular job and handle day-to-day living, he found there were no more easily achieved victories. No longer were people praising him for his easy achievements. Now, there was only the long pull of adulthood that all parents know only too well.

Jason wanted excitement, the quick thrills of his youth. He described his life as "too normal, too healthy, too organized."

By getting everything so easily for so long, Jason had become convinced that he was a golden boy, that life was golden for him. (He was indeed a very gifted and lucky kid.) Unfortunately, adult life was not as simple or as easy as he thought. So he escaped to drugs.

WHAT COULD JASON'S PARENTS HAVE DONE DIFFERENTLY?

Jason's parents gave him love, discipline, attention, and direction. But he was born with a personality that could not handle stress. Hindsight is always a great deal better than foresight and, looking back, Jason's mom realized that perhaps rather than smoothing out stressful situations for him, it might have been better to let him deal with the pain of them. Maybe they should have encouraged him to greater challenges in school and in sports, since a little bit of losing might have been a lot better in Jason's case than all his easy victories.

Jason simply hadn't developed any psychological muscle. Although he was working and married, he just wasn't prepared for the ennui, the reality of hard work and long days without end that is a part of most adult lives.

Yes, Jason's parents might have set up situations to teach him how to deal with his inability to handle stress, to see that he really wasn't golden. But since Jason seemed to be maturing quite well, it would have taken parents with the wisdom of Solomon to realize what he needed.

Our purpose in telling this story is not to make anyone feel that a situation like this is hopeless. Rather, it's to point out that sometimes there may be nothing that parents can do. Or that what they should do is so subtle that they don't stumble onto it until it really is too late. In other words, you're not to blame if you don't understand or if the problem isn't under your control.

Jason's parents simply weren't at fault. They gave love, discipline, and guidance. They did all they could.

BEWARE OF PLAY

Children who love to play are wonderful. But children who love *only* to play can be heading for trouble—whether it's in the form of choosing play before work or deciding that school, sports, and life in general are so easy that it's all play. Children have to be made to realize that life is not just made up of rewards. There is also hard work and some boredom and some pain.

14

The Teenage Bully

When children are young, their parents' authority comes from several sources. For one thing, adults are simply bigger than children and, if necessary, they can carry off the toddler who refuses to leave the playground or take away the toy two youngsters are fighting over. For another, parents completely control the purse strings, so young children depend entirely on them for food, clothes, and shelter. In addition, young children don't have enough independent information or the intellectual sophistication to challenge their parents' arguments.

But adolescence erodes those sources of authority. Teenagers are often as big as or bigger than their parents, so physical discipline is no longer feasible. Teens also have other sources of money, such as part-time jobs, so they can buy things and go places without their parents' permission. What's more, they're far more likely to challenge—or even dismiss—their parents' reasoning.

Teens may feel they no longer have to do what their parents say; they may even feel they can now boss their parents around. The result can be a teenage bully.

BOYS WHO BULLY THEIR MOTHERS

Bullying can be a particular problem between teenage boys and their mothers.

When the boys were small, mom may have had no trouble enforcing discipline. But now that they are big, in the back of their minds is the knowledge that they are taller than mom, they weigh more, they are faster, and they are a heck of a lot stronger. Why, then, should they let her push them around?

It's a question of who is the parent and who is the child. Mom is the parent and the teenager is still the child. But the teen doesn't want to be a child anymore. He wants the power he sees available to an adult.

If the teenager has experienced normal pain in growing up, he may realize that mom is only doing what she sees is best for him. He will understand that the discipline she imposes comes from love and concern, and he will accept it.

But quite likely, the teenager retains a great deal of his infantile narcissism. Mom has protected him from normal pain all these years and now, as a teenager, he really doesn't have a clear picture of mom. He doesn't see her as a feeling human being who can be hurt. She is simply his provider who, through her discipline, is now trying to restrict the freedom he feels should be his.

Since the narcissistic son sees the world as revolving around him, he can visualize no need for restrictions. Therefore, mom becomes a nuisance or, what's worse, the enemy. When she gets strict with him, since he can think of no good reason for obeying, he tends to ignore her. As she tries even harder to maintain control, he's apt to let her know who's the more powerful of the two.

Cindy

Cindy had two boys who were only a year apart. They were ideal children, she felt, until they became teenagers. Then, about the time the younger hit thirteen, they turned into real terrors.

Since Cindy worked, she felt the boys should do their fair share of the work load. She set up some simple rules. They were:

1. Do your chores before you watch TV or go out.

2. Complete whatever you start—don't leave any tools out and don't leave a task unfinished.

The chores themselves were minimal—washing dishes, taking out trash, putting clothes in the washing machine. It would only take each of the boys about a half hour to do his work. But the boys simply did not want to do it. At first their resistance wasn't direct, but the jobs didn't seem to get done. Cindy noted several techniques they used:

"I Forgot."

The boys would do the chores only if they were reminded. After reminding one son to take out the trash for the fourth time in as many days, Cindy decided that this was simply a game he was playing. So she wrote out his chores, had him sign the list, and tacked it to his door. But when she came home the next day, once again, the work hadn't been done and she had to remind him to do it.

"You mean ALL of it?"

This was particularly the technique of the older boy. He might wash the dishes in the sink, but leave the pots and pans. When Cindy came home, she would tell him he wasn't finished. He would look at her with great surprise and say, "You mean you want me to wash those, too?"

"I did it."

After a while the boys began to blatantly lie, particularly the younger of the two.

"Did you do your chores?"

"Yeah."

"Then how come the garbage can in the kitchen is still full?"

"Oh, that."

If Cindy confronted the child by asking why he lied, he would resort to an excuse such as, "I didn't know you wanted it done" or "I forgot."

"There, I did it."

Yet another technique was to do a bad job. The dishes were all stacked up neatly, but when Cindy looked at them, they were dirty. They had been washed without care.

When the older boy, who favored this technique, was asked about the dishes, he would reply, "You wanted them done. They're done. If you don't like the way I do them, do them yourself."

Cindy decided that there had to be some consequences for not doing the work or for doing it badly. If the chore wasn't done as it was supposed to be, then she imposed an additional chore. But the more Cindy insisted that the boys do their chores, the more confrontational they became. They added new techniques:

"There's nothing you can do to me."

When Cindy would say something like, "You didn't do the dishes, so now you have to do the dishes *and* mow the lawn," the response would be only a shrug. "Sure, I'll do the lawn. I like mowing. I'll get to it as soon as I can."

The child refused to be affected by the consequence. It was as if he were saying, "You can't do anything to me. I'm more powerful than you. I'm only doing this because I've decided to go along with what you say."

"Mom's a bitch."

Eventually, it wasn't just the chores, it was everything. The boys wouldn't do anything Cindy asked. In addition they would swear at her under their breaths. And they would do all they could to bully her. She began to feel like a prisoner in her own house.

Going to the Counselor

Cindy was at the end of her rope. She would come home from work and nothing would be done, but the boys would be watching TV. She would have to wait until her husband, Ron, came home and then complain to him. He would speak to the boys and they'd get up and do the work. But they wouldn't do anything for Cindy.

She decided it was time to get help, so she sought out a counselor. The counselor told her, in essence, "You worry too much about the boys' behavior. Boys will be boys. Don't worry about whether or not they are responsible. They'll eventually outgrow it. Ignore it."

But that approach didn't work. If the boys needed something, they might let her bribe them into completing a task. But short of that, they were like independent souls floating around the house. And she was taking constant verbal abuse from them.

Finally Cindy decided that she had a right to set standards for behavior in her own home. If she wanted chores done, then that's the way it had to be. If she wanted to be addressed respectfully, then that's what they would have to do.

Last, and most important, Cindy decided that she was not going to let two teenagers bully and intimidate her into abandoning her expectations for them, particularly when the chores she wanted done were so minimal.

One day when Cindy came home and found the boys sitting in front of the TV, she went over to it, turned it off, and told one to take out the trash, the other to do the dishes.

The boys just looked at each other and smirked. Then the younger went over and turned the TV on again.

Cindy turned it off and repeated her request. When the younger reached forward to turn on the TV, she slapped his hand and told him, "Don't touch that dial again."

The boys, however, were used to running the show. The older boy stood in front of Cindy, blocking her from the TV while the younger turned it on. Then, smiling, they sat back down to watch television.

Cindy may have lost the battle, but she had not lost the war. That night she carefully explained what happened to Ron. She told him, "I'm going to take some drastic measures. It's become a power struggle. Who's in charge here, them or me?" Cindy told Ron she realized that she might make the boys very angry at her, might even make them hate her for a while, but that she couldn't let them bully her any longer. Ron said he'd back her all the way.

The next day when the boys came home they found the TV set was gone. Cindy had sold it. Also the refrigerator was empty, as was the pantry. The boys' clothes and things had been taken and stored elsewhere, leaving their rooms bare.

Needless to say, when Cindy came home from work, the two boys were angry and demanded to know what was going on. She told them she had nothing to say to them until they spoke to her in a respectful tone of voice. She went back out the door, got in her car, and drove around for half an hour.

When she returned the boys were waiting. She could tell they were seething, but they spoke respectfully. The minute they began to shout or use a swear word, she'd turn to leave.

They maintained their control.

Cindy told them that from now on they would have to earn everything around the house by doing their chores. If she came home and the chores were done, she'd take food she had bought out of the car and make dinner. If they weren't done, she and Ron would eat out and the boys wouldn't have any dinner.

She'd give them just the clothes they needed to wear to school. If they stacked these neatly in their rooms, then slowly she'd give them back the rest of their clothes and things.

After a month, if they behaved themselves, she'd think about getting a new TV. And one other thing. This was just between her and them. They could complain to Ron if they wanted to, but ultimately they would have to answer to her to get the things they wanted.

It took a while, but eventually Cindy did turn things around. Now she has two well-behaved teenagers who know their place.

THE EFFECT ON MOM

Cindy's victory was not without a price. She said, "I was astonished to find in myself such strong feelings of conviction about what I have a right to demand. I was a child of the sixties, a liberal who walked in street marches for civil rights. I believed strongly in freedom. And I shudder to see the conservatism emerge in me. It's as if I've become a different person."

Ultimately, Cindy got rid of the bullying that was intimidating her by insisting on what she felt she deserved and by refusing to be walked on. However, this didn't happen until she was so frustrated that she was willing to risk losing the love of her children.

To some parents, Cindy's actions might seem drastic. Those parents might be more comfortable locking up the TV rather than selling it, for instance. Each parent must decide what he or she can live with. Whatever you decide, make it logical and something you can carry through. Think the solution over carefully from beginning to end. Decide what is the worst possible thing that could happen if you did take a specific action. If you can live with it, then do it. You'll respect yourself in the long run.

THE ROLE OF GUILT

Although it took Cindy a long time to admit it, she had allowed things to get so far out of control because she had reacted from guilt.

Each time the boys showed disrespect for her, she interpreted it to mean that they didn't love her. If they didn't love her, she felt, it was because she wasn't giving them enough love.

Thus, she was caught in a no-win circle. The more the boys bullied her, the more she felt she should show them love. They saw this only as weakness and bullied her all the more.

It was only when she put her guilt aside and decided her own peace of mind was important that she was able to take effective action and win the respect of the boys.

A rule for Cindy and those of us like her is that it's important to love ourselves and be more selfish long before things get this bad. We must realize that maintaining our parental authority over our children doesn't mean they'll stop loving us.

Cindy's rough action with her boys did not cause them to hate her in the long run, although the immediate effect was anger. Ultimately, in part through Cindy's help, the boys began to see that the universe was not at their beck and call. When they realized this, they accepted the fact that they would have to do chores. Eventually they even admitted that their behavior was terrible and that Cindy had done the right thing.

THE 10 PERCENT RULE

When dealing with bullies, let 90 percent of the behavior go, but insist on compliance with 10 percent.

This is a military tactic. It stems from the fact that you can't be everywhere all the time. The idea is to pick a target and stick with it.

Whatever you select, whether it's cleaning up the room, washing the dishes, or another chore, define the behavior you expect and accept nothing less. In addition, as Cindy demonstrated, there must be immediate and important consequences for the child for non-compliance.

Cindy would be hopelessly lost if she tried to insist every minute of the day that the boys do things her way, speak respectfully, and otherwise carry on as they had as children. But she could easily demand that they complete thirty minutes of chores.

The miracle is that once you've established a beachhead, the rest of the behavior tends to improve on its own. Once you set down the rules for that 10 percent and the teen sees that you will enforce them, the bullying behavior seems to disappear in the other 90 percent. If a person is going to be a bully, they have to be a complete bully. They can't be a bully 90 percent of the time and a wimp the other 10 percent.

By insisting on 10 percent compliance, you can avoid turning your home into a jail and yourself into a police officer. At the same time you make the problem into something you can handle.

If a teen bully is making your home life miserable, then you have to effect some changes. It's your home and you have to feel comfortable living in it.

In most circumstances it's just a matter of acting like an adult. Bullying is a child's game that requires two to participate. If you refuse to be a part of it, the child has to think of you as a parent.

PART 3
Guilt-Proofing Your Parenting

You've taken two major steps toward getting rid of that disabling burden of guilt you've been carrying: You've learned how to recognize a range of factors that can influence your teenager's behavior and to cope with the effects. You've learned to identify different types of problem behaviors and picked up some tips about how to deal with them.

Part III is the final stage in your journey toward guilt-proof parenting. A short quiz that lets you tell how *you* would handle situations like those we've discussed throughout the book will help you determine just how big a role guilt plays in your parenting. Then we'll give you seventeen guidelines to help you become a better parent by diminishing that role.

15
The Parenting Quiz

When you face a problem with your teenager, how much does guilt affect the way you handle that problem? Can you act effectively, or are you paralyzed by guilt? Do you do what's best for your child, or do you get distracted by trying to figure out what you did wrong?

This quiz is designed to help you determine just how much guilt interferes with your parenting. Pick the solution that most closely fits how you might handle each problem. At the end, calculate your score to find out just how guilt-proof you really are.

1. Your teenager stays out for three nights without telling you where she was. When she comes home, she says she left because you are too strict. You:
   a. send her to a counseling center to "cool" her off and give you time to figure out how to deal with her.
   b. let her come home without any consequences.
   c. let her come home and work with her to establish new rules she'll find more acceptable.
2. You've been sick for three days and barely able to keep food down. You ask your fifteen-year-old son to stop by the pharmacy for your medicine on his way home from school. He balks, saying he's already been late for his play rehearsal three times because he's had to take his bike. You:
   a. remind him of the times he's asked you for favors and insist that he go.
   b. pay the pharmacy to deliver the medicine.
   c. go to the pharmacy yourself and give him a ride to rehearsal on the way.
3. Your daughter comes home with a B- on a paper you helped her write. She is really upset about the grade and blames you for it. You:
   a. tell her that's the last time you'll help her if she has that kind of attitude.
   b. decide silently never to help her again.
   c. tell her you're sorry about the grade and go talk to the teacher about it.
4. Your child has been caught shoplifting. Another teen got away, and your son won't tell who it was, even though he would get a lighter sentence. You:
   a. make sure he understands the consequences, then let him live with them.
   b. try to coerce him to tell.
   c. go before the judge to ask for leniency.
5. Your daughter didn't do her chores all week. Your contract with her says she can't go out on Saturday when she doesn't do chores, but this Saturday night is an honors

banquet where she is to get an award. You:

    a. keep her home from the banquet but send a note of apology.

    b. send her, but ground her the next Saturday.

    c. send her anyway because she was to receive an award.

6. Your teenager just called you a name in front of company. You:

    a. tell the child she will not be allowed to talk to you that way and you'll discipline her later.

    b. smile at your friends and say, "Isn't that just like a kid?"

    c. feel embarrassed that your friends have seen how little control you have over your child.

7. Your son's bicycle was stolen and you have just replaced it. Despite your warnings, the first day he has it, he leaves the new bicycle on the street with no lock. You:

    a. return it to the store and get your money back, then tell your son he'll have to earn money to buy his own bike.

    b. leave the bike on the street and hope it gets stolen.

    c. put it in the garage and give your son another lecture.

8. You have just found out that a close neighbor gave your thirteen-year-old money for a movie she knows you object to. You:

    a. go over and talk to the neighbor about the problem.

    b. tell your child not to go over there any more.

    c. forget the entire thing.

9. Your child has been cited for having alcohol in the car while driving. He admits he's guilty. You:

    a. take the car away until he goes to trial.

    b. lecture him, but allow him to drive until time for the trial, then let the judge decide the punishment.

    c. tell the judge the liquor was yours so your son doesn't lose his license right before the prom.

10. Your daughter throws a fit because you won't let her go out with a friend you disapprove of, saying she only has

this one friend because you just moved. You:

    a. tell her the answer is still no, and take her to a youth center to meet other kids.

    b. say no this time but tell her she can bring the friend over to the house tomorrow.

    c. let her go and hope it turns out okay.

11. Your teenager is having trouble with a teacher, and you know that it is definitely a personality conflict. You:

    a. leave her in that class and discuss ways she can cope.

    b. go talk to the teacher to try and smooth things out.

    c. remove her from the class with no questions asked.

12. Your son is supposed to do the dishes, but for the third time this week it's almost time for bed and he hasn't touched them. You:

    a. take the dishes out of the sink and put them on his bed.

    b. do them yourself and confront the issue later.

    c. do them yourself and forget about it.

13. Your daughter has been late for school every morning this week because she won't get up in time. On Friday, when she's late again, she begs you to write her an excuse. You:

    a. refuse.

    b. write the excuse.

    c. give her a lift even though it means you'll be late for work.

14. You know your child has stolen money from your wallet. You:

    a. confront her and request the money back. If she has already spent it, you take the money from her next allowance.

    b. get angry and call her names.

    c. forget it and increase her allowance so she'll have enough money.

15. You've been planning for three months to get away for a weekend. Just as you're about to leave, your son tells you he hasn't saved enough money for his class ring and annual and it's due tomorrow. Giving him the money means

you can't afford to go away. You:

    a. go on the trip and have a good time.

    b. go on the trip, but feel upset and worried the entire time.

    c. give him the money and postpone the trip.

How to score the quiz:

0 points for answer a

1 point for answer b

2 points for answer c

If your score is:

25-30 GUILT-RIDDEN

    Guilt colors almost everything you do and may be interfering with your ability to be an effective parent. When facing decisions like those described here, stop to consider whether you're really at fault and, if not, what the real problem is. Always be on the lookout for guilt creeping up on you.

20-24 GUILTY UNTIL PROVEN INNOCENT

    You're not completely guilt-ridden, but you have probably bought the cultural myth that you are to blame for all the things your child does wrong. Reject the blame and stand up and fight for your rights to be a guilt-free parent.

15-19 GOLDEN MEAN GUILT

    You are an average guilty parent. You need to trust your instincts more and not be overly influenced by others. You're doing fine, so give yourself a pat on the back, and don't give up on your efforts to become completely guilt-free.

10-14 GUILTLESS

    You have occasional twinges of guilt, but for the most part you've survived a lot of the societal pressure and are being an effective parent. Keep it up, and don't berate yourself for those few lapses.

9 or   GUILT-PROOF
less   Hurrah! You're doing it right most of the time. You know that you're not responsible for everything your child does, and refuse to let guilt run your life. Both you and your teen are better for it!

16

Seventeen Steps to Guilt-Proof Parenting

After reading this book, you know a great deal more about guilt in parenting than you once did. You know that children are naturally narcissistic, that they haven't yet learned to empathize with others or to deal realistically with the world. You understand that children can be quite clever and manipulative when they want their way. What's more, you should see that letting them have their way is often bad both for them and you. You got it! Now, here's what you need to make it work.

In this chapter, we're going to give you seventeen guidelines to help you put these new insights to work in your day-to-day life. They'll help you avoid the common pitfalls of parenting and will make you feel less helpless. If you use them, you should find that you are getting rid of your guilt, removing those feelings of regret, and, most important, dealing effectively with your teenage children.

1. Work at Being Happy Yourself

When Dr. deGarcia was reading parent books shortly before she first became a mother, she came across this statement by Dr. Benjamin Spock: "If the parent is not happy, the child is not going to be happy."

There's a lot of truth in this. We all know that children model their parents' behavior and that they listen, to some degree, to what parents tell them. But nothing rubs off more than attitude. If you're pleased with what you're doing, with your parenting, with your work, with your marriage, with life in general, your children will pick up on those feelings. They will tend to be happy.

On the other hand, if you're not happy with yourself, more than likely your children will internalize bad feelings.

Make your own physical, emotional, intellectual, and spiritual well-being your first concern. After that everything fits into place more easily.

2. Take Care of Your Relationship with Your Partner

For parents with partners, a second goal becomes paying close attention to loving and caring for each other. When a therapist works with dysfunctional families, the first thing he or she does is try to strengthen the parents' relationship. If this is done, the relationship with the children will fall into place easier. If children see a split camp, they work to drive you apart in order to get their way.

Take care of your relationship after yourself.

3. Trust Yourself

Most parents do a pretty good job. They didn't have children to hurt or destroy them; they have their best interests at heart.

But what happens is that the culture undermines parents. All the books are so conflicting in their advice, and parents don't have anybody to support them. When they turn to others for help, very frequently they get blamed.

As a result, parents have to be self-reliant. They must do things based on their gut-level feelings. Therefore, the rule is that if a parenting decision feels right at that level, then you should be secure in thinking that it probably is. After all, if you're reading this book you probably are a person who is constantly trying to improve and grow. Trust yourself.

4. Love Your Children, But Learn to *Detach*

If there is any one clue to dealing with children that's most helpful, this is probably it. The most effective parents are those who have learned to detach themselves. The least effective are those who can't or don't know how.

Love your children and be really close to them. Put your arms around them and give them lots of hugs. But the minute they try to force you to give them their way or to try to harass you, emotionally detach yourself from them. Think of it as if you were on a job and a customer started yelling at you. If you were going to be effective at your job, instead of yelling back, you would detach yourself. You would become very, very businesslike with the customer. You would be calm so that you didn't feed the hysteria and escalate what was going on.

The same thing applies to children. When a child starts to get emotional or wants his or her way, or starts to call you names or embarrass you in public, or whatever, detach.

If you don't detach and instead react from the heart, you immediately get down to the child's level. You're back in the playground screaming and taking sides. You've stopped being the adult among kids. You're all kids, and the only resolution is to yell, scream, cry, pout, and hit.

Keep your dignity and your adulthood. It's important to remember that you are the parent and they are the child. Detach. Put your heart away and start using your mind. Don't forget who you are. Breathe deeply and remember you are a model for your child and you are teaching her or him lessons in life.

You can begin by saying in a very calm voice, "I love you, but you can't have the car keys. I love you, but no more cookies for you tonight. I love you, but you can't go on a camping trip with your girlfriend."

Detaching yourself means using your intellect instead of your emotions. When your child demands his or her way, use a slow, calm, businesslike tone.

No, it isn't easy. The majority of the time, it's easier to just give in to a teen's tantrums. And the easy way is usually quick, dirty, and apparently successful because the child goes away happy. But in the long run, if you take the easy way, your child will become increasingly selfish.

Try handling tantrums like this. Tell you teen, "You don't talk to your friends like this and I don't want you to talk to me like this. So I'm going to leave the room (or I'm just going to go away from you) and when you're ready to talk and we can talk in a non-emotional manner, then we'll do it. But as long as you're using this tone of voice or these words or these kinds of tactics, I'm not going to be here."

That can be very, very effective. Dr. deGarcia uses that with all of her own kids and none of them talks back. When the parent walks out of the room and refuses to engage, teens quickly come to understand they aren't going to get anything until they talk to the parent like a human being.

It's easier if you've used this technique from the beginning, but if you're already in a situation where you've let it go, don't give up. Just do the same thing—walk away and refuse to engage if they're being abusive. It will take longer, but eventually they will come around.

Remember, the reason they are talking to (yelling at) you is because they want something. They can't get it if you don't listen (engage), so their self-interest makes them act differently. You are part of the human race. Detach yourself and make them treat you like a person.

5. Never Negotiate When You're Tired or Busy

All the parent guides tell you to be consistent. If you're not consistent, your child will not understand. The trouble is, it's really difficult to be consistent. When you're preoccupied or tired, you can't always remember what you said before, so you say something else. You're inconsistent.

There is a way out of this trap. The key is to let the children know that when you are tired or busy, they are not to ask you for anything. If they do, the answer is automatically no. If they complain, you can explain, "That's just the rule."

If you're on the phone and they ask you for something, the answer is automatically no. If they ask for something when you're fixing the toaster and you're frustrated because it's not going well, the answer is no. If you're shopping or doing anything whatever and they interrupt and ask for something, there's no negotiation, no nothing. The answer is automatically no.

That stops them. It keeps them from interrupting you and from taking advantage of your weak moments.

But beware, the kids won't like it. This rule will get in the way of their wishes. So after you make the rule and stick to it, expect things to initially get worse instead of better.

You may go through three to six months of a lot of anger because nobody wants to lose an advantage. But, if you keep this program up, eventually they are going to fall into line because you are going to refuse to deal with them unless they talk to you and work with you and deal with you in a humane manner.

They like to talk to you when your mind's distracted by something else because they have learned that's a great way of getting what they want. They will complain that you're ignoring them, that you don't love or care about them. But eventually they will start to get trained so that they know that if you've said you're tired and you've put up a sign on your door not to bother you or whatever, the answer is automatically no. So they won't ask.

6. Slow Everything Down

Children like to speed everything up and ask for immediate action. They say, "Hurry, I've got to know right now because everyone's going" or "I've got to have the money because there's someone outside." The answer in this situation is always no. Make that the rule.

Always ask for space and time. Tell them, "I will give you an answer, but you will have to give me about ten minutes to think about it." This is particularly hard if you're an unassertive parent, because you may have a hard time standing up to your kids.

But it's critical to give yourself enough time to think. If you react without taking time, the chances are that the answer will be the wrong one. Slowing things down also involves changing the pacing of events between you and your children.

For example, children are always popping up with a note to be signed a minute before they have to leave for school. You don't have time to read the note, let alone make a decision about what it says. And the child is hammering away, "I've got to go! I've got to go. Hurry up, the bus is coming!"

Tell your children, "If you want notes signed for school, give them to me the night before. I will not sign them in the morning."

Of course this takes some determination on your part. If the child brings it to you in the morning and says, "I'm sorry, I forgot last night. Please sign it now; I've got to go," you have to detach yourself, smile empathetically and say, "I love you, but I won't sign it because you didn't give it to me last night."

Expect an outpouring of pleading and anger. The child will tell you of all the terrible consequences that will happen to him or her because *you* aren't signing the note (because it's *your* fault).

Maybe there will be some terrible consequences. But if you don't sign, it will teach the children something else. It will teach them that if they want anything from you, they'll have to give you enough time to think it through calmly or they pay the penalty. After a while, they'll get trained.

Another area to slow things down in is shopping. Often the kids will come running up with "I want this or that" statements just as you're going out the door to do the shopping.

Put a shopping list up on the refrigerator. When you're out of something or they want something, they have to add it to the list. If it's not on the list when you go shopping, then they don't get it. That slows them down.

Slowing them down is important because when you go shopping, if you're not in a good psychological frame of mind, you'll buy too much or you'll give in to their wants. But if they have to write it down on a piece of paper, then you can budget and decide whether or not you really can afford (or want) to get it.

Again, they won't be happy, particularly if you have been the type of parent who has gone out at 9 P.M. on a Sunday looking for typing paper for a child who needs to finish his or her term paper by 8 the next morning.

If you shop only once a week, it means that for one week they will be inconvenienced, that's all. It teaches them that your time is important, too. It helps you to keep the budget and yourself in control.

Slowing things down teaches respect, responsibility, and reason—three Rs that are important for your children.

7. Write Out a Contract for Each Child

Each child, no matter what age, should have a written contract that states exactly what you expect them to do, what rewards they get, and what happens if they don't keep the agreement. The hardest part is what to do if they don't do as agreed. Don't think in terms of punishments. Think in terms of lessons to be learned and of them taking responsibility for their actions.

For example, perhaps you have a teenage girl who slams the door all the time. You keep asking her not to do it, but she ignores your requests. Part of the contract you create, besides including chores such as washing the dishes or whatever, will be, "You will not slam the doors." A consequence of slamming the doors could be, "If you continue to slam doors, after a week the door to your room will be removed."

What you're doing is not punishing, but trying to teach lessons in life. The lessons should be relevant to the problem. They should also be constructive in the sense that they teach the child that there are significant consequences for continually doing something that they are not supposed to do.

The contract is important because it makes clear exactly what your expectations are. Never underestimate your children's ability to misinterpret what you want done. They don't see things from your viewpoint, they only see things through their own perspective. Consequently, until you write it down they may really not know exactly what you want.

8. Make Rules Very Specific

As we've seen, children have their own interpretations of what parents say. Therefore, it is vital to be as specific as possible.

For example, if you say a child is "grounded," what exactly do you mean? Does that mean staying exclusively in the house or does it include the yard? What about phone calls and friends coming over? What about the TV?

One mother told her daughter she was grounded and had to stay in the house and not have any friends over.

The next day she came home and there were four of her daughter's friends in the swimming pool. Her daughter was in the house, leaning out the window, talking to her friends.

She hadn't gone out of the house and the friends hadn't come in. In the daughter's mind, she was abiding by the rules. The mother had to be very specific. No friends in the house or in the yard. No talking to friends through windows or doors. Not even the toes of any friends anywhere on the property!

The more specific you are, the better. Remember, kids aren't going to be concerned with your intent. What they are listening to is exactly what you say. If you don't say it, then as far as they are concerned, you didn't mean it.

9. Write Details Down

Don't trust your memory—your children don't. For example, you tell a teenager it's okay to go somewhere, but that he has to come home at 11. He comes in late and says, "You said midnight."

Suddenly you're into a full-blown argument about what time you said. The fact that the child is late gets put aside and it becomes a matter of discussing your failing memory. That won't happen if you write down the time.

If you have more than one child, it's increasingly hard to remember what you said. Did you say it to Elise or to Marc?

Establish a notebook or a 3×5 card file someplace so that when you tell a child that they can or cannot do something that's a little bit out of the ordinary, you write it down.

10. Break Negative Patterns

Sometimes you and your kids play the same scene over and over again. It's as though you are trapped on a stage forever repeating the same play.

For example, whenever you come out wearing something new or different, your child is critical of what you are wearing. You then reply that you like what you're wearing and she shouldn't be so negative. She says it's just her opinion, but she doesn't want to go shopping with you today if you're going to wear that outfit. She would die of embarrassment if her friends saw her.

Suddenly you two are off and running in an argument that gets repeated and repeated. It happens over and over again every time you wear something new.

What you've got is a pattern. Both you and the child have trained yourselves to respond in set ways. As soon as you come out with new clothes, the pattern begins.

You can tell if you're in a pattern if the same negative emotional situation about the same subject occurs three times or more.

It's up to you to break that pattern; your child is probably not mature enough to do it. The first step is to find out exactly what the pattern is. This is harder than it may seem. Someone outside the little play may easily be able to pick out the characters and the plot. But from within, you may be blind to what's happening.

As soon as you go through a negative emotional incident that feels familiar, write down exactly what happened. Start just before the situation began and write down exactly what happened and how you reacted.

When you've done this for several incidents, you should be able to clearly see the pattern. Now it's a fairly simple thing to change. Simply write out a new scenario. Write out a new and different reaction to use when your child starts the "old record." Break the pattern. Smile, laugh, grab and kiss her, stand on your head, thumb your nose. Do something different and, hopefully, unexpected.

Then the next time you come out wearing a new blouse and your child says how old-fashioned it looks, say something such as, "Thank you. I'm really glad you're interested in what I wear."

The child, who has been ready to proceed with the next stage of the patterned argument, suddenly realizes that you missed your cue. The play can't continue. She has to improvise and the pattern is broken.

Try practicing it and working with it so that you learn new behaviors. You can say almost anything as long as it breaks the pattern. Remember, it takes two to be set up. If you constantly find yourself in the same negative emotional situation with the child, you're part of the set-up. Get out of it, now!

11. Don't Give Your Children Ammunition

Never tell your kids all the things about you that are negative or that need to be improved. Remember, they are your children, not your friends or confidants.

Kids are so immature that when they get angry and want to win, they will bring up anything they know will help them. They won't realize how hurt you can be by what they say. What's worse, once you've told them something best left unsaid, they'll bring it up again and again.

It's a lot harder for a loving, caring parent to use guarded honesty with his or her children than to always tell the whole truth. But in the long run, it's better both for the parent and for the child.

12. Talk to Parents Who've Survived Their Children's Teen Years

When parents are having difficulties with their children, they naturally turn to their friends. But many times parents have friends who are the same age group, the same religion, the same ethnic group and so forth. Chances are they are going through the same problems. Therefore, you don't get constructive advice. You just get mirroring. The blind leading the blind.

But parents whose children are ten or more years older than yours can be truly helpful. They not only will have gone through what you are experiencing, but they also will have had the opportunity to see what happens over time. They will have put distance between themselves and what you're going through and, therefore, can talk about it with a clearer perspective.

When you talk to these older parents, you'll see that there *is* life after children, that children do grow up and become people you want to be around. They can give you some insights to make your current hectic life a little more philosophical and bearable.

13. Get a Support Group

Try to get a couple other parents to meet with you at least once a month just to talk about everyone's problems. Just knowing that you're not alone can be helpful. Also, techniques that other parents have discovered may prove helpful to you.

A support group can be essential for a single parent, particularly a single woman. We wish it weren't true, but our experience has shown that people tend to pay far less attention to a single mom. When a man comes along, people sit up and listen.

If you're a single mom, you might want to consider getting someone from your support group to go along with you to parent conferences at school or to court appearances or to other such "formal" meetings. If you take a male, it can give you more stature with authorities. (Of course, you may prefer to go alone and insist that authorities learn to deal with single moms. If so, be aware that you may have to overcome some resistance.)

14. Be Careful When Selecting a Therapist

You need to see a therapist when you feel you can no longer solve the problems, when the old methods are not working, and when things seem overwhelming. Remember, a referee or an objective opinion from an outsider may give you a different way of looking at your situation.

However, just as all doctors and car mechanics are not the same, all therapists are not going to give you the same kind of results.

Selecting a therapist can be tricky. A *Reader's Digest* article in 1986 suggested, and we suggest, that you get the address of the Professional Association of Therapists in your state. Get the names and addresses of the therapists they suggest. Another method is to call your county, city, or state mental health organization and ask for referrals. Finally, your priest, rabbi, or minister will usually have some good referral suggestions. But above all, interview three to five different therapists until you find one who is compatible with your goals and values.

When you go to these therapists, find out if they are *pro-parent*. Be sure they have children or are realistic about children. Ask them a few questions about their experiences with their children. Do not be afraid to interview them. Listen closely to see that the therapists are "real," that they talk about the foibles of their own children or lives. (Do they seem human?)

Beware of therapists who only tell you how wonderful their own children are and who never mention their children's problems. These people may have a romantic, unrealistic viewpoint about children. Chances are they won't be helpful to you.

You need someone who has been in the trenches and has learned to cope with children. If your therapist hasn't experienced this type of pain and conflict with his or her child, or is afraid to admit it to you, be cautious. You want an ally and this might just be a fault finder.

An inexperienced therapist or a fault finder can make you into a great scapegoat. If this happens, your child may never have to face his or her responsibility in the situation. Since there are usually no innocents in a problem situation, this can be very detrimental.

Remember, this person is going to be a very influential factor in your child's life. Be sure that he or she has values similar to your own.

15. Get Second Opinions

If you do seek professional advice, take it all with several grains of salt. If you go to the school or to the psychologist or to some other "authority" and you get some advice that just *doesn't feel right to you,* stop. Before acting on that advice, go out and get three other opinions.

You may be astonished to discover that someone else has a totally different (sometimes totally opposite) perspective. The rule here is that for loving, caring parents, doing something that does not feel right may not be right. You wouldn't rush off for major surgery on the basis of a single doctor's evaluation. Don't operate on your children unless you likewise get second opinions.

16. Don't be Afraid to Try a Temporary Separation

One of the most common misconceptions among parents is that they are admitting failure if they send their child away to live with someone else for a while. The guilt of sending away their son or daughter can be so overwhelming that most parents won't even consider the idea.

That's unfortunate since a period apart can be extremely beneficial for both you and your child. It can be a useful experiment in maturing and a time of growth. The simple act of separating from the child for a period of months can all by itself clear a whole raft of problems that might otherwise be insoluble. Sometimes the kids just have to get away to cool off.

Consider the alternative. It's been Dr. deGarcia's experience that if things get bad and the parent doesn't do something like create a new positive environment for the child, then he or she may run away, get pregnant, start taking drugs, or do some other desperate thing to escape—which can be much worse than what would happen if the parents sent the child away for a while.

Sending the child away for a time may be the most positive thing you can do. Just think of it as taking a vacation from each other. It does not mean that you failed. After all, there is the possibility that while the child is away, he or she may discover that you are a great parent! All that it may take is the perspective that distance offers.

When to Send a Child Away

How do you know *when* it's time to consider sending a child to a new environment? Generally if the child constantly does not follow direction and harrasses you, and if you're beginning to lose control, it's time.

From an emotional perspective, it's time when you feel hopeless because you've tried everything else and all you've gotten is negative results. Don't be swayed by those occasional moments when you hold each other and cry and promise that it's going to get better. If it's not getting better, love may simply not be enough. You may have to break the negative response patterns and the negative reactions to get things on a positive footing. Additionally, spending time apart allows you to see if it's your problem or if it's something outside the family.

Where Can You Send Children?

Some parents simply send their children off to a boarding school or a relative. Living with the other parent in a divorce situation is sometimes helpful, as long as you set the limits. For example, you may agree that the child can live with the other parent for one year. That gives you a rest.

Usually kids will get much better when they are sent away because in the new environment they are treated much more objectively. Don't always hang on and think that nobody can raise your child but you.

17. Discuss Emancipation With Your Teen

If you've got a "mid teen" (thirteen to seventeen years old) who's not following rules, who is not doing anything that seems right and who's telling you that they can't wait to get out of the house, let the child know that emancipation is an option.

The emancipation laws allow you to declare the child independent. He or she is no longer your legal or financial responsibility. They are legally on their own.

Many teens think this is what they want. But faced with the reality of it—looking for a room to rent, a job, setting up a budget for whatever money they have—they find out whether they are really grown up. When you mention that they could move out, suddenly they have to start thinking about what it's really like to be independent and "free." More than likely, they will suddenly see the advantages of the family.

IT ISN'T EASY

All of the suggestions in this chapter, while constructive, nevertheless can be very difficult to do. The reason is, quite simply, that most parents don't want to have their children dislike them. You want to be loved, and many of these suggestions are going to make your children angry with you at least part of the time.

But it's important to understand that being a parent means you're going to be hated or strongly disliked 30 percent of the time. If your children are happy with you 100 percent of the time, then you're not doing your job, you're not a good parent. Parents who are afraid to do anything because it might cause their children to become angry are paralyzed by fear (and guilt, if they take any action). You don't want to be that kind of parent. If you are, you are doing your child, yourself, and your society a great injustice.

BUT IT'S WORTH IT!

If you work at these rules, you can begin to have a better life with your children almost immediately. What's more, you'll discover that your children will start treating you like a human being and they will even begin to respect you.

The key behind all these guidelines is that they help the child see you not as a slave, not as only a provider, but as a flesh-and-blood person. As soon as they begin to see you this way, they start to mature and become better people. And your life becomes a lot easier.

You want a better life for your children and for yourself. So fight back. Love them *and* put them in perspective.

Start today. It is never, never too late.

CONCLUSION

After writing this book, we're struck by the fact that some readers may be thinking, "Is it really that simple? If I'm aware of my child's narcissism and manipulations, are my problems virtually solved?"

Of course it's not that easy. But as we've noted before, it all begins with awareness. From there it takes hard work. But awareness leads you in the right direction.

YOU HAVE TO DO IT

Remember, if you are a guilt-ridden parent who always takes on all the responsibility for your children, your children will never learn from their mistakes. They will go into society and fail because no teacher, boss, spouse, or anyone else will take what you have allowed them to dish up to you.

If you do not step out of the partnership that is creating the problem and make your children see you as a person and help your children deal with the negative part of growing up and help them to take responsibility, you will cripple them.

If you do not make your children see their part in the problem, they will never give up their self-centered thinking. They will be like the grasshopper in the child's story sitting on a rock in winter playing on a fiddle and freezing to death (while the ants worked hand-in-hand to build their nest) singing, "Oh, the world owes me a living. . . . la de da, la de da. . . ."

But if you learn to put your guilt aside and ask your child to live up to his or her responsibility, if you can assess a situation fairly without automatically blaming yourself and instead looking for the real cause, you can help your children grow into responsible, caring adults.

MOVING FORWARD

The suggestions in this book are just that. You need to read more, talk to more people and adjust what you discover to your own lifestyle and temperament. We hope we got you started, made you aware, and helped you see the circumstances you are in a little differently. The changes come by putting one foot in front of the other and moving forward.

We hope we've given you the encouragement to get started.

INDEX

Page numbers italicized in this index refer to material covered in Case Studies.